POSITIVE
POPULISM

POSITIVE POPULISM

*Revolutionary Ideas to Rebuild
Economic Security, Family,
and Community in America*

STEVE HILTON

CROWN
FORUM
NEW YORK

All rights reserved.
Published in the United States by Crown Forum,
an imprint of the Crown Publishing Group,
a division of Penguin Random House LLC, New York.
crownforum.com

CROWN FORUM with colophon is a registered
trademark of Penguin Random House LLC.

Library of Congress Cataloging-in-Publication Data
Names: Hilton, Steve, author.
Title: Positive populism : revolutionary ideas to rebuild
    economic security, family, and community in America /
    Steve Hilton.
Description: New York, NY : Crown Publishing, [2018]
Identifiers: LCCN 2018013750 (print) | LCCN 2018015977
    (ebook) | ISBN 9780525575597 (e-book) |
    ISBN 9780525575580 (hardcover)
Subjects: LCSH: Political participation—Social aspects
    United States. | Populism—United States. |
    Decentralization in government—United States. |
    Political culture—United States.
Classification: LCC JK1764 (ebook) | LCC JK1764 .H557
    2018 (print) | DDC 320.56/620973—dc23
LC record available at https://lccn.loc.gov/2018013750

ISBN 978-0-525-57558-0
Ebook ISBN 978-0-525-57559-7

PRINTED IN THE UNITED STATES OF AMERICA

Book design: Jen Valero
Jacket design: Lucas Heinrich
Jacket photographs: (Steve Hilton) Courtesy Fox News Channel;
(paper textures) thinkomatic/iStock/Getty Images, NikolaVukojevic/
iStock/Getty Images

10 9 8 7 6 5 4 3 2 1

First Edition

To my mother, Hajni Hilton
Thank you for all the possibilities you created for me.
I know it wasn't easy.

CONTENTS

INTRODUCTION   *1*

THE POPULIST ECONOMY   *13*

1 SECURITY   *17*

2 OPPORTUNITY   *48*

3 FAIRNESS   *72*

THE POPULIST SOCIETY   *93*

4 FAMILY   *97*

5 COMMUNITY   *120*

6 COUNTRY   *139*

THE POPULIST GOVERNMENT   *163*

7 LOCAL   *167*

8 ENTREPRENEURIAL   *185*

9 ACCOUNTABLE   *199*

CONCLUSION   *217*

Acknowledgments   *221*

POSITIVE
POPULISM

INTRODUCTION

THIS IS AN INVITATION for you to participate in the next revolution: the return of power back to the people, just as the Constitution intended.

Why is a revolution needed? Just one shocking fact tells the story. If you take inflation into account, in 1972 the average American worker earned $738.86 a week. In 2016, the figure was $723.67 a week. Forty-four years and a pay cut of 2 percent. That is why we need a revolution.

But why a *populist* revolution? Why must it return *power to the people?* The case I'll make to you in this book is that the institutions and policies that shape today's economy, society, and government overwhelmingly benefit those at the top—not just the famous "1 percent" but more like the top 20 percent; that working Americans have been left out of the many great advances made by this elite in the last few decades; and that the ladder into the elite is mostly broken.

I want to show you that this state of affairs—intimately linked to the transformative trends of our time, globalization and technology—is not inevitable or something outside our control, like the weather, but is instead the result of deliberate policy choices made by the elite who benefit from them. Those policy choices are an ideology in their own right, shared by a ruling class of Republicans and Democrats, conservatives and liberals, and we can describe that ideology as elitism. Elitism's defining characteristic, and the central reason for its failure, is the concentration of economic and political power in the hands of the few, not the many.

That's why we need a specifically *populist* revolution.

The result of the 2016 presidential election and Great Britain's "Brexit" vote to leave the European Union five months before were the first tangible signs that such a revolution may be possible. In both cases, members of the ruling class—in all mainstream political parties, in business, in academia, in the bureaucracy, and in the media—were united on one side; yet voters chose the other.

But those votes themselves were not the revolution. It's what happens next that matters. Will the election of Donald Trump, the Brexit vote, and other irruptions of populist sentiment at the ballot box turn out to be vocal but insubstantial phenomena that leave the underlying power structures unchanged? Or will we see a decisive shift of power from the elite to the rest of society?

This book sets out ideas for long-term change that would bring about that power shift, and thereby deliver the positive promise of populism: to improve the standard of living and quality of life for working people. To strengthen the ties of family, community, and nation that bind us, ties that have become so horribly frayed of late. To make government more accountable and responsive. And to do all this in a way that is open and welcoming.

But populism will only be *positive* if we—you—make it so.

We need to reclaim the revolution from those who would take it in a different direction. Until now, populism has been defined by the people who don't believe in it. It has been characterized by elites on the left as "nativist," even "racist"; by elites on the right as "unconservative" or "anti-capitalist." The people's anger has horrified the elites on all sides. And no wonder: the technocrats, bureaucrats, and corporatists from Wall Street to Silicon Valley, from Brussels to Davos and back to Washington, DC, sense a threat to their power. They may not really understand the revolutionary impulse but they do see it as a terrible impertinence.

Regardless, there are good reasons for the rage at today's establishment: insecurity in the present, anxiety about the future, and impatience for change. It adds up to a whole lot of anger. But anger without an agenda leads to self-pity and further frustration. That's why the populist revolution needs to be fashioned into a coherent and positive political philosophy, one that understands and respects today's anti-elite sentiment but channels it away from any dark ends toward constructive and lasting transformation of our economy, society, and government.

We all know—or think we know—what populism is against. Now it's time to spell out what populism is for. That is the aim of this book, to show how positive populists can help remake America with radical reforms rooted in the uplifting and unifying idea at the heart of the grassroots rebellion: *people power*. That is, of course, the idea at the heart of America itself. In that sense, by advancing the aims of Positive Populism we reclaim the American Revolution, too.

So it's time to attack the terrible concentration of economic and political power that has disfigured and divided America, undermining faith in our institutions, in democracy, even the rule of law. It's time to put power back in the hands of the people. For this to happen, that power must be wrenched from the clenched fists of the insiders and the plutocrats and the assorted hangers-on of our comfortable ruling class.

And by the way, I know what I'm talking about. I'm one of them.

I DIDN'T START OUT like that.

I grew up in a small town in the south of England. My parents were Hungarian immigrants; they met while working in the kitchen of a cafe at London's Heathrow Airport. My father (who had once been the goalkeeper for the Hungarian national hockey team, winning an Olympic medal), walked out on us and returned to Hungary when I was four. My mother earned what she could as a clerk in a shoe store and later in the "typing pool" (younger readers: Google it) of a bank's head office. Later, she met my stepfather, also Hungarian, who had arrived in Britain as a refugee after the 1956 Soviet invasion. Back then he was a teenage boy living within a day's walk of the Austrian border. He still recalls the cries of his neighbors: *The Russians are coming!* He, his brother, and some friends ran for freedom. Some didn't make it. Hungary's democratically elected prime minister was imprisoned and executed. My stepfather was sent to England, where he found work on a construction site and over the years built his own small construction business.

We were not a particularly political family: politics was rarely, if ever, discussed. But I did pick up a couple of things.

I learned of the calculated cruelty meted out to my maternal grandmother by the communist authorities after her daughter— my mother—settled in the West. She was fired from her job as a teacher and publicly denounced as a bad parent and citizen in front of all her colleagues and pupils. That's what authoritarians do.

I learned too about basic values: you had to work hard to get anywhere. The worst thing in the world was to be a "layabout." And on this topic I do recall a hint of politics: I remember hearing that in 1980s Britain, when I was coming of age, the left-wing

Labour Party was for the "layabouts" and the Conservatives' Mrs. Thatcher was for working people. In that—and in her resolute determination to win the war against communism—she was our champion.

Now: Imagine how I felt when just a few years later I found myself walking through that famous black door of No. 10 Downing Street to deliver a briefing packet that I had personally prepared for the prime minister, Margaret Thatcher. Or when shortly after that I was on hand to assist in her conversation with a visiting party dignitary from newly democratic Hungary, after the fall of the Soviet Empire.

How did that happen? Well—the same way most working-class people rise: education. I won a scholarship to an amazing high school, Christ's Hospital, which transformed my expectations and ambitions. From there I made it to Oxford University, where for the first time in my life I was rubbing shoulders with the elite. And before you knew it, I was one of them.

But I've never forgotten where I came from.

I HELPED REBUILD AND MODERNIZE the Conservative Party in Britain after it had spent more than a decade in the political wilderness. I then worked as a strategist and policymaker at the heart of British power in 10 Downing Street as senior advisor to Prime Minister David Cameron.

Once a supporter of Britain's European Union membership, by seeing up close the regular—almost daily—countermanding of the British government's policy decisions by the unelected bureaucracy in Brussels (the headquarters of the EU), I had come to realize the astounding degree to which the United Kingdom had ceded control over its national destiny. Words from America's Declaration of Independence provide a resonant parallel: "The history of the present King of Great Britain is a history of repeated injuries and usurpations, all having in direct object the establishment of an absolute tyranny over these states." For "King of Britain" read EU; for "these states" read Britain . . . and you've pretty much got it. The EU had become an ever-expanding, increasingly opaque, and endlessly intrusive institution. Governance was moving further and further away from the British people, their families, and their communities.

During the EU referendum in 2016, I broke with the Tory leadership and argued that the United Kingdom should become a real democracy again—a nation in which citizens live under laws made by the leaders they elect to represent them. My stance led to a difficult and very visible falling-out with Prime Minister Cameron—not just my former boss, but my longtime friend and the godfather to one of my children.

The United Kingdom's Brexit vote on June 23, 2016, confounded the establishment's predictions. It was truly the swelling of a populist wave.

But the election of Donald Trump five months later was the tsunami.

The shell-shocked elites really should have seen it coming. Over the past few decades, anonymous technocrats, bureaucrats, and corporate apparatchiks built a governing axis between Big Government and Big Business. In turn, politicians—buoyed by donors, charmed by lobbyists, and courted by the media in exclusive watering holes like Davos, Brussels, and Washington—forged a bipartisan consensus backing globalization, automation, centralization, and uncontrolled immigration.

Power shifted from people to unelected overlords and moved from nation-states to international bodies like the International Monetary Fund, the World Trade Organization, and the EU. In the economy, the rich got richer and working people saw their incomes go down and their jobs go away. Meanwhile, in our society, the human ties of family and community that bring us together were ripped apart, with nothing but arid techno-commercialism to take their place.

Economic injustice. Social breakdown. Disillusionment with democracy. These underlying causes of the populist rebellion are worsening, and the elitists seem to have no positive answers. Populist upheaval has instead been met with dismay and condescension by global elites, emotions echoed by their propagandists (and dinner party companions) in the media. They focus on the negative: vilification of immigrants, anti-Semitic incidents, violence directed toward opponents and minorities. These phenomena remind us that populism can indeed turn sinister. But that's all the more reason to offer a strong and clear populist philosophy that is positive. We can agree that globalism isn't democratic—without becoming isolationists. We can agree that a nation is not a nation unless it can enforce its borders—without being racist. We can agree that cultural norms such as two-parent families and a work ethic play a role in lifting people out of poverty—without being bigoted.

Here's what Positive Populism means in practical terms. It is a pro-worker economic agenda designed to lift the living standards and reduce the economic anxiety of the majority of working families whose incomes fell as economic power was concentrated in the hands of the elite. It is a social policy agenda that aims to repair our torn social fabric, focusing in particular on the breakdown of family and community. And it is an agenda for political reform that is all about decentralizing power and fighting corruption. Those are the themes of the positive populist movement, and this book.

In Part One we describe the Populist Economy, with *Security*—economic security—as its foundation, in Chapter 1. You will find new ideas for boosting jobs and wages—but for reforming healthcare too, since the impact of our broken healthcare system is felt most keenly in the household budgets of working Americans. Chapter 2 examines *Opportunity*, focusing on ways to give people the skills they need to flourish in the twenty-first century, including revolutionary ideas to transform schools and worker training. In Chapter 3, *Fairness*, we tackle the concentration of economic power that has allowed corporate CEOs and Wall Street chieftains to make their own rules. Among other ideas you will see a bold and completely original approach to competition and antitrust.

Part Two is devoted to the Populist Society: how to repair our torn social fabric and strengthen its three key elements: *Family* (Chapter 4), *Community* (Chapter 5), and *Country* (Chapter 6). This section will take on some taboos—for example, strongly advocating for the role of marriage in family stability, with specific new ideas for helping reverse the long-term trend of family breakdown. And it will offer a strong and passionate challenge to the "globalist" ideology, addressing some of the biggest issues facing America, including immigration and the threat from China.

Finally, in Part Three we explain how Positive Populism can reform our democracy to make it more *Local* (Chapter 7), more *Entrepreneurial* (Chapter 8), and more *Accountable* (Chapter 9). The Populist Government ranges widely: plans to shift power not just to state and local government but to neighborhoods, as well as the most comprehensive and draconian assault on corruption and the Deep State that has ever been proposed.

Taken together, the ideas set out in the chapters that follow really do represent a revolution, one in which people would win the power to control their destiny. Of course, in certain ways, people today have more power than ever before. Power over what to read, watch, and listen to. Power to buy what they want when they want. Power to summon a car, or a meal, or someone to help with their chores. Power to connect with anyone, anywhere, at any time. But they don't see a corresponding rise in empowerment when it comes to public policy and the structures that are supposed to support a flourishing life.

People are rebelling against government and business institutions that for decades have been allowed to get bigger and bigger, promising efficiency as the benefit of scale. But now these institutions have grown too complex to operate with humanity, too arrogant to prioritize the common good, and too powerful for regular citizens to control. Unless you already have the economic and social capital to play their game, you are left behind.

Under the current cronyist system—which poses as an entrepreneurial capitalist one—Big Government is steered by Big Business, which funds and lobbies politicians with the expectation of protection. Increasingly, though, the shoe is on the other foot, with Big Government leveraging its influence to demand money from Big Business. Either way, whether it's corruption or extortion, it's more like feudalism than capitalism—with voters and consumers as the serfs. And now Big Tech, which once promised liberation, is fast achieving overlord status as its power becomes more and more concentrated.

Elitists see centralization as benign, even necessary. They are technocrats, foolishly convinced that they can, and should, keep running things from on high. The positive populist, on the other hand, believes in the diffusion of power: truly competitive markets, localism. And by appealing to universal values and ambitions, Positive Populism seeks to lift up the most disadvantaged citizens and those struggling to keep pace with the rapid changes all around.

Instead of rejecting the new populism, freedom- and progress-loving people in office and those seeking office should embrace it and make it work for good. Positive Populism represents the kind of optimistic, encouraging view of people power that inspired Thomas Jefferson and the first generation of Americans who declared independence and launched the revolution that forever changed the world.

THERE'S SOMETHING ELSE THAT'S SIGNIFICANT about Positive Populism as a political philosophy. It is pragmatic, not ideological; inclusive, not tribal. Its aim is to solve problems using the methods that are most likely to work, whether or not they offend the "true believers" in America's two old parties. Conservatism once claimed the mantle of pragmatism, but today it seems that dogma has taken over. Liberals and Progressives claim the mantle of compassion, but their results tell a different story. Let's be honest, both old parties have failed working people for years. In the nearly half century since the early 1970s, under Republicans and Democrats of all different kinds—from conservative to moderate to liberal— the rich got richer while half the country got poorer. Literally.

There's no rule that says the right are for the rich and the left are for the workers. When I was coming of age politically in England, to the frustrated disgust of the intellectual elite it was the Tory daughter of a middle-class Grantham grocer whom the working class trusted—not Labour, espousing wealth redistribution and Keynesian economics. In many ways, Prime Minister Thatcher delivered on a populist agenda, with reforms designed to put economic power in working people's hands—for example with her spectacularly successful effort to widen home ownership. She recalled in *The Downing Street Years:*

> [W]e were embarked upon a great programme of ambitious social reform to give *power to the people.* Those we wanted to empower were not just (or even mainly) those who could afford their own homes or private schools for their children or who had large investments, but those who lacked these advantages. (p. 572)

Margaret Thatcher understood that all people, not just the rich, want and deserve independence and opportunity. Now, in America, we need a new people power revolution, a positive one. It must not smash things up simply to vent: serious thought is needed over which institutions should be left untouched, which should be fixed, which should be torn down, and what should be created anew. The positive populist's target is the dehumanizing bureaucratic institution—Big Government, Big Business—not the people who work inside them. As Americans begin to cut these institutions down to size and make them more responsive to the people, we should ask at every turn, "Is this reform *more human, or less?*" A postideological focus on solving problems at the human level gives us the best chance of answering the big questions that we wrestle with on a societal level:

How do we generate faster economic growth while reversing the wage stagnation that has hurt all but the richest over the past few decades?

How do we control immigration without hurting our economy, which depends so much for its success on innovation and the free market of ideas?

How do we help the victims of globalization and automation without casting off the many benefits of trade and technology?

How do we solve our fiscal crisis without slashing essential services and hurting our nation's most vulnerable?

These are the hard problems of the modern age. Surely America, of all places, can solve them? This country has a populist core.

Its reputation for individualism is second to none. Its participation in organized religion is an overwhelmingly positive hallmark. Europeans may mock Americans for their cheerful civic-mindedness, but they ought to be envious of it. No country in the world is, at its core, more populist than the United States.

During the 2016 presidential campaign, I attended both party conventions in my role as then CEO of my political crowdfunding start-up, Crowdpac. My wife, Rachel, was traveling abroad for some of that time, so I decided to take our children, Ben and Sonny, with me. In Philadelphia, we visited the National Constitution Center.

Having studied politics, philosophy, and economics at Oxford, I recalled debates about the differences between America's founding documents and the British system, which has no written Constitution. But standing there in Philadelphia with my sons, contemplating our new life in the United States, I was moved to tears by the center's exhibits and dramatic reenactment of America's founding story. The American people took power back from a remote, bureaucratic empire. What a remarkable idea. America's is the first written Constitution in the modern world, and a model for all other nation-states. The best nation in the world, founded on the most beautiful idea in the world: liberty under the law.

And it all begins with "We, the People."

THE
POPULIST
ECONOMY

To the elite, the economy means dividends, interest rates, stock performance. They read the *Wall Street Journal* or the *Financial Times*, watch Bloomberg television, and breathlessly opine on trade flows, political risk, and other macroeconomic indicators. To them, the economy is a game to win, a turn at the blackjack table. Salaries are measured in hundreds of thousands, maybe millions of dollars; wealth by the size of your property.

But for most people the economy is better represented by lyrics from one of my favorite songs while I was growing up in England, "A Town Called Malice," by The Jam:

> Struggle after struggle, year after year . . .
> To either cut down on beer or the kid's new gear
> It's a big decision in a town called malice. . . .

Struggle after struggle, year after year: that is the grim economic reality for so many working Americans, regardless of whether the economy has been growing or is in recession; whether the stock market has been booming or crashing. The economic reality has also been grim regardless of which party has been in power. On the right, the obsession has been with "free markets" and "spending cuts," no matter the practical impact on people's daily lives. On the left, it's been about "redistribution" and "intervention," with more focus on looking compassionate than actually making a difference. On both sides, ideology has driven out pragmatism, which is hardly a sustainable solution to long-term, structural problems.

Working Americans don't want massive government intervention in the economy, as is commonplace in Europe. But neither do they want to be left alone in an economy tilted in favor of the rich elites. American workers are the most ingenious in the world, but they have to be equipped to succeed. It's time for their interests to come first, rather than the interests of the owners of capital and the already-rich.

A pro-worker policy agenda has three essential elements.

First, practical steps to give every American economic security. This does not mean lurching into some massive socialist welfare state. But we cannot expect workers to succeed if they are frightened of going bankrupt all the time, including over healthcare expenses. Second, a new effort to spread economic opportunity. We need a completely different education regime, one that gives students the skills they need for the new economy—and one that helps workers make transitions throughout their careers. The third element is action to bring fairness to our economy. Crony capitalism has got the better of the free and fair marketplace, and that needs to change. America was built on unparalleled entrepreneurial energy but is being defeated by lumbering incumbents that crush potential competitors.

The kitchen-table issues of old are still the kitchen-table issues of today. Healthcare, education, and jobs are basic stuff—but today we need revolutionary ideas to build an economy that favors working people. Positive Populism has to start there.

1

SECURITY

FOR THE ELITE, the word *security* immediately evokes foreign policy debates. But for working Americans, it's all about economics.

I know what economic insecurity feels like. My father left when I was four, and my mother couldn't support us. She herself had been raised in a stable, professional-class family back in Hungary, so it must have been humiliating for her to ask for financial help from them after she fled the Iron Curtain for the supposed riches of the West. But she did what she had to do. My early memories are of life in a damp, dark basement apartment—and then another on the top floor of a building, with a rusting iron balcony that today would likely be considered a death trap. My mother worked in a shoe store, so I would always go to a friend's house after school. I envied the warmth and comfort of their middle-class family home.

Our situation improved when my mother met my hardworking stepfather, who is still her partner after forty years. (Monogamy certainly contributes to security.) As soon as I was allowed to, I wanted to earn money. I signed up with a temporary employment agency in search of odd jobs, like washing up in restaurant kitchens. My income wasn't necessary to cover our basic needs, but early on, I learned to associate money with independence and control over your own life.

Before Oxford, I spent my gap year working for a construction company up in London: I'd take the train from my hometown of Brighton every morning, along with all the other commuters. I was only sixteen years old but I loved the feeling of "going to work." I started out doing odd jobs in the office but ended up a junior project manager, coordinating work on various construction sites. While I was at university, I would always work temporary clerical or manual jobs—whatever I could get—during the breaks. Again, it wasn't to survive: our family income qualified us for a "full grant" from the government for living expenses during university, and in those days the state paid all tuition fees, too. I just wanted that extra security.

All the way through my twenties I was constantly worrying about money. I still recall the panic I would feel at the seemingly eternal bank overdraft, or when my friends and I would approach an ATM and I was unsure if I could withdraw even the minimum offered by the machine.

Still, because of the sheer luck that life bestowed on me—a mother who always put me first and did everything in her power to give me the opportunities she never had (and which my cousins left behind in Hungary didn't have), a steadfast stepfather, the priceless gift of a world-class education, and more recently the hard work and spectacular professional success of my wife, Rachel—financial security is not something that I worry about today, for myself or my children. But I know this much from personal experience: if you don't have economic security, if you don't know how you'll get through the week financially, if you can't see any way to pay the basic bills—nothing else matters. It takes over your life and becomes a question of survival.

That's what life is like today for somewhere between a third and half of our fellow citizens. Just one single emergency, like an unexpected medical bill or car accident, can pull the rug out from under more and more Americans who have been living paycheck to paycheck, worried about their health insurance, stagnant wages, and their role in an increasingly automated economy. That's why economic security is the number one issue in America today, and the foundational issue of Positive Populism.

It's not a partisan political issue: during the sixteen years of George W. Bush and Barack Obama, with various changes of political control in Congress, half of American households saw their incomes go down (with the poorest seeing their incomes go down the most). It made no difference who was in charge politically; the rich got richer and half the country got poorer.

But you can go back even further than the turn of the century. One startling example: the 80 percent of American workers with production and nonsupervisory roles brought home an average weekly wage of $723.67 in 2016, according to the Economic Policy Institute. That's about 2 percent less than they did in 1972, when the inflation-adjusted average was $738.86. In forty-four years our economy delivered working Americans a 2 percent pay cut. Surely it is evident that something serious is wrong: something that we can't just ascribe to the "failed policies" of one side or the other in our political game. Isn't it obvious that American capitalism itself has gone haywire?

It's time to question the fundamental assumptions that have undergirded our economic debates for decades. We have been told—and by the way, I myself (in my former role as a political advisor) have done my fair share of telling—that the centerpieces of the elitist economic agenda, those well-worn articles of faith for both parties in recent decades—globalization, automation, immigration, and the centralization of policy-making in the hands of technocrats—are improving our lives. By some measures, they are. But look at the measures that matter most. The fundamental expectations of the American middle class have been shattered by the elitist consensus. We grew up thinking that our children would have a better life than us—no longer a safe assumption. We believed that a job would always be there for everyone who wanted one—no longer true. We were told that if you worked hard you could provide a good, secure foundation for yourself and your family.

Well, what a hollow promise that is for most working Americans today, who struggle to afford the basics of a decent life on the inadequate and often unpredictable wages of a typical job. The beginning of the twenty-first century, notes political economist Nicholas Eberstadt, was a turning point: "the Great American Escalator, which had lifted successive generations of Americans to ever higher standards of living and levels of social well-being, broke down around then—and broke down very badly."

The response of the elites is instructive. They talk about today's brutal, merciless, sink-or-swim economy as if it were some kind of inevitability, fashioned by forces beyond anyone's control. But collapsing economic security is not inevitable. It is the direct and intended result of elitist policy, designed, built, and maintained by the people at the top: the CEOs and the Wall Street wheeler-dealers; the technocrats and bureaucrats; the bankers and the accountants and the management consultants—and of course their political stooges in Congress and elsewhere throughout the system.

We keep hearing that a "flexible labor market" is the future—that the jobs are there for people who are willing to learn new skills, to move to where the work is. The elitist ideologues instruct the lower orders: *Why, you must adapt! You must be willing to chase employment opportunities across the country. You need to understand that you will have to make multiple career changes throughout your life to keep up with the forces of supply and demand.*

Much of that is true—and will be discussed in the next chapter. But we have to ask: why didn't the elites think about all this before they took a wrecking ball to millions of people's economic security? Why didn't they make even the slightest preparation for the wrenching transition that they engineered? Why are they only now, decades into their experiment, starting to realize that people have been hurt—and badly?

It is of course because the victors in the elitist economy were blissfully ignorant of the lives of its victims. Who benefits in a flexible labor market? The wage earner who must move every few years, who keeps being told they're no longer needed and must become someone else, who can never plan for anything because they never know how many hours' work they will get and how much they'll be paid, who has a mortgage that's underwater, school-age children with all the costs that entails, who can't count on healthcare and other benefits from their employer anymore, whose spouse has to work two or more jobs on the side just to keep the show on the road?

No; the winners from our much-lauded "flexible labor market" are the CEOs and company shareholders. They are the big businesses with a fleet of lobbyists in Washington. They are the successful entrepreneurs with capital set aside. And this is the problem with the elitist agenda: too much cold economic theory, too little warm human empathy.

If there's one piece of evidence that most powerfully tells this story, it's the connection between worker productivity and wages. For decades after World War II, as America's economy grew and became more productive, workers shared in that growth. Productivity and wages grew in line with each other. But then something went wrong. The economy continued to grow and become more productive, but wages actually went down or stayed flat, even as economic growth and rising productivity boosted the incomes of the richest Americans who own businesses instead of just working for them.

To appreciate the scale of the problem—and the revolutionary scale of the change we now need—it's vital to understand exactly *when* things started to go haywire, the point when incomes began to stagnate. It wasn't the financial crash and the Great Recession; it wasn't the dot-com bust; it wasn't the sharp downturn of the early 1980s. It preceded all those disruptions.

This is not an economics book and the reader will not be subjected to an incomprehensible parade of graphs and statistics. But do please look at this chart. It shows more vividly than any words possibly could that our economic malaise goes back, in fact, to the early 1970s. Inflation-adjusted wages for the typical American worker have been falling or flat since 1972—that's four decades of stagnation.

Workers produced much more, but typical workers' pay lagged far behind
Productivity and typical worker's compensation, 1948–2013

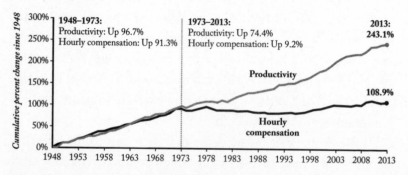

Source: Bureau of Labor Statistics, Bureau of Economic Analysis

The inflection point coincides with a huge change in economic policy, and it was all to do with the concentration of economic power. A new doctrine, originally advanced by economists at the University of Chicago and then widely adopted in all three branches of government, argued that competition in the economic marketplace was less important than outcomes for consumers. As long as corporations were operating "efficiently," they should be allowed to get bigger and bigger and bigger—whatever the impact on workers or local communities. Since that dramatic break from centuries-old American tradition, there have indeed been "efficiencies." The economy has more than doubled in size. Productivity has risen by over 70 percent. The incomes of the top 20 percent of earners have gone up by 150 percent; the top one percent—well, you know the story, up by more than 400 percent since the early seventies. But the vast majority of the working people of America have not shared in that progress. At all.

Their growing sense of economic insecurity is the primary force behind the populist surge in America, and it is the reason voters in 2016 rejected the mainstream elitist candidates in both the Republican and Democratic parties. The reality of mass economic insecurity must be confronted for the grave and long-standing crisis that it is. Looking ahead, America needs an explicitly pro-worker policy agenda to restore economic security.

A pro-worker agenda is the foundation of the Populist Economy. It means taking on the callous elitism that fetishizes disruption with a shrug and a lecture: "Sorry, this is the way the world is going. Suck it up and get with the program." At the same time, we must challenge the vindictive populism that pretends "it's all the fault of the rich, of big business. Tax them more and everything will be okay." Business—good business—is the heart of any successful economy, including a populist one. My stepfather began as a wage-earning laborer on a construction site but eventually began his own business as a general contractor who could pay wages to others. I've started businesses throughout my life: back in the United Kingdom, Good Business, a corporate responsibility consulting firm, and the Good Cook, a community restaurant; here in America, Crowdpac, a tech start-up aiming to put political power back in the hands of the people.

The positive populist favors reform that puts aside resentment or ideology and instead delivers practical solutions to help working people prosper in today's economy. That's why the Populist Economy has to start with a plan to end economic insecurity—because if people don't know how their medical bills will be paid, if they can't count on ever seeing a wage increase, if they can't afford the basics of a decent life, or be confident that the economy will sustain them in old age, they won't even be in a position to seize opportunities to rise, something we should want for every American. Economic security is not a luxury, it is a necessity.

And it is something that America, the richest country in the world, can amply afford.

THE 2008 FINANCIAL CRISIS showed us that Big Government can certainly afford to help its friends (and donors). The elite were quick to step in to help those institutions deemed "too big to fail" but passive when it came to the plight of those who are small. In other words, the working people. Not a single executive from any of the companies that caused the global financial crisis has been prosecuted, but when an average American makes a poor decision, she can anticipate economic and bureaucratic punishment for years afterward.

Think of all the working Americans, with no intentions of defaulting, who signed up for mortgages and credit cards without full consideration of the future interest rate increases that were in the fine print. And now a growing number of working-class Americans, eager for a steady income, waive their negotiating leverage and future mobility by signing their employer's noncompete clauses—clauses originally intended to prevent commercial secrets from following the highest flyers to a competitor but now widely applied in such monstrously inappropriate settings as fast-food workplaces.

Some elitists might believe that with better budgeting practices and greater impulse control, those struggling financially could build up capital and become economically secure with no help from government. That is wishful thinking. Many Americans live close to the edge, with few if any savings. In a 2015 study by the Federal Reserve, 46 percent of those polled said they didn't have enough money to cover a four-hundred-dollar emergency. But at the same time 69 percent of respondents reported they were either "living comfortably" or "doing ok."

Perhaps they don't realize they're only one emergency away from the 31 percent who aren't doing okay. That anxious third is likely suffering from cognitive overload, in a way someone with the focus and free time to read this book has probably never experienced. Furthermore, let's remember that these are people who are working—often harder than most. When we talk about economic security we are not talking about people who have opted out and settled for a life on welfare. We are talking about the working poor—not necessarily captured in official poverty statistics but poor nonetheless.

Princeton psychologist Eldar Shafir and Harvard economist Sendhil Mullainathan, who have studied the effects of scarcity on the brain, suggest that the working poor's stress levels lead to poor decision making, which further entrenches them in poverty. Depleted of both money and time, they're captured in a state of "bandwidth poverty," and thinking about or planning for the future is all but impossible.

Worse, because of the toxic effect of stressful situations on developing brains, the children of the working poor often suffer from continuously elevated hormones that affect their own habits (for example, the exercise of self-control in school, diet, criminal behavior), which inhibit their own upward mobility.

People with "bandwidth poverty" end up making bad decisions that haunt them for years to come. Many low-income single parents, often minorities and immigrants, rely on "payday loans"— short-term credit with an extremely high APR—to cover regular recurring expenses. Some move in with a partner who is not committed to family stability (or worse, is abusive) to reduce expenses. Once these acts of desperation are under way, the effects are difficult if not impossible to reverse.

When working Americans face an emergency, they likely don't have access to the networks and institutions that the upper tier does. Consider how much more economically secure the elite are, thanks to their ability to work the system. It's likely they were coached by their own parents—as soon as they became employed or parents themselves—to authorize automatic payments for recurring bills like rent and insurance from their bank accounts, where their wages are directly deposited by their employers or clients. The high premiums they pay in case disaster strikes are just another necessary expense in the lives of upper-middle-class people, in case their house burns down or their car is wrecked, or they are physically incapacitated by an illness.

It's also likely they own property, and homeowners in good standing on their mortgages are usually able to bridge a crisis by taking out a home equity loan. They're twice benefiting from the system in this case: the interest on their mortgage provides them with a sizable tax deduction every year, and the interest they pay on the home equity loan is also tax deductible.

Even middle-class people who aren't homeowners find themselves better equipped for emergencies than the working poor, because often they have some asset they could sell to avert a crisis: a car or some stocks or a piece of jewelry. Not an ideal situation, but it's not the same as stepping in quicksand.

Finally, let's not underestimate the social capital that economically secure people can tap into: very often, they have family members whom they can approach for a loan—however awkwardly, as my mother had to do when I was young. Frequently enough in America, they may be members of a religious or civic organization that will see them through an emergency.

Given all the ways in which families and life situations drown so many people in stress and reduce their decision-making capacities, and given that all this is going to get worse as the economy moves toward more episodic working and away from the kind of long-term full-time employment that was the norm in the past, the positive populist looks to ideas that will help reduce the specific fears that contribute to economic insecurity. And that's not just about income. For most working people, the biggest manifestation of economic insecurity is not "below-par growth" or "wage stagnation." Yes, those things are vital, and we'll get to them in a moment. But the most urgent driver of economic insecurity for most people is actually healthcare. That's why it's the first of our three big ideas to combat economic insecurity.

1. REDUCING THE BURDEN OF HEALTHCARE
ON PEOPLE AND BUSINESS

Medical issues and health coverage play an enormous role in to-day's economic insecurity. For a start, healthcare affects people's employment decisions—whether they change jobs or move to a different state with different coverage. In 2016, around 15 percent of Americans didn't have enough money for necessary healthcare and/or medicines, over 40 percent struggled with medical bills, and even 12 percent who were *insured* faced healthcare insecurity. Those conditions cannot sustain a globally competitive superpower.

According to the National Bureau of Economic Research, "soaring health insurance premiums do more than swell the ranks of the uninsured. They boost unemployment, push more workers into part-time jobs, and force employees to sacrifice wages and other benefits just to retain some measure of coverage."

One of the leading causes of personal bankruptcies in the United States is medical expenses. This is unfathomable to me, as someone who grew up in a country where you didn't even have to think about paying for healthcare. Britain's National Health Service covers all residents and is free at the point of use (although of course funded by taxpayers).

It's far from perfect, I assure you. In my twenties, I sustained a leg injury and was told by a local doctor that a deep-vein thrombosis had developed. At the nearest NHS hospital I was triaged and told that DVTs could result in a fatal blood clot: "It's only a matter of hours." I returned to the waiting room, desperately worried. And then the clinic director announced they were short-staffed, and everyone waiting would need to go home and return tomorrow! Luckily I had a friend whose father was a doctor in private practice, and I phoned him late at night (and lived).

Many others have not been so fortunate. A succession of well-documented scandals in the NHS left patients mistreated in disgusting and degrading ways that in some cases led to their death at the hands of the very institution that was supposed to care for them. Less dramatically, there are daily stories of neglect, incompetence, bureaucratic obtuseness, and of course the famous delays for treatment. And the outcomes are often poor: the UK has the worst cancer survival rate in Europe for example. Despite all this, however, many British people will tell you not just of their regular frustration with the NHS, but their immense pride in it too, a pride that is widely—almost universally—shared.

Here's the reason: while the United Kingdom's "single payer" system is certainly not the panacea its defenders claim, it does have the singular benefit of completely removing healthcare as a factor in economic insecurity. Whatever else happens to them, the Brits, regardless of wealth, simply don't have any of the financial worries or bureaucratic headaches associated with healthcare in the United States: the poring (and often agonizing) over insurance plans, the destabilizing impact of an unexpected health incident, the fear of moving to a different job, the widespread risk of personal bankruptcy. All of that is compounded, of course, when it comes to children. Could there be anything more stressful or agonizing than worrying about how to pay for healthcare for your child? It's an all-consuming burden for any American parent (and there are many millions in this category) whose child is not covered by Medicaid or the Children's Health Insurance Program. What cruelty, to engineer a system that makes parents worry that they can't save their child if they develop a serious illness.

You don't see the burden on business, either. It's astonishing to me, as the founder and CEO of a small business in America, that I had to get involved in the healthcare of my workers. It not only feels inappropriate and intrusive on a personal level, but it's a massive regulatory and financial cost, too. I thought America was supposed to be the land of free enterprise. And yet here we are with the government forcing businesses to take responsibility for their employees' healthcare! Incredible.

Less obvious—but just as pernicious—is the impact on our culture and way of life. It's easy to complain (and many do, including me) about America's ridiculous risk-averse culture, the endless overwrought health and safety warnings, the waivers, the lawsuits. But do we ever stop to consider that the healthcare system is a huge driver of all this? When so many people can't afford to pay healthcare costs, it's not surprising that there's no such thing as an accident anymore: you always need to find someone to blame in order to cover the cost of medical care.

None of this is to say that single-payer healthcare is right for America, however. The mistake that is often made in the American healthcare debate is to assume that the only way to reduce the burden of healthcare on people and business is through a gargantuan, state-run single-payer bureaucracy like the United Kingdom's National Health Service. Many countries offer residents universal healthcare without resorting to a single-payer system like Great Britain's or Canada's: Germany, Switzerland, New Zealand, Ireland, Israel, Australia, and Singapore are all examples.

There are a number of ways to achieve the benefits of guaranteed universal health coverage while retaining—indeed enhancing—the benefits (such as greater medical innovation, higher quality of care, and much shorter wait times) that can be produced by a competitive private healthcare economy. It all comes down to separating the two very different elements of the system: health coverage and healthcare. Muddling them together is what has hindered real, practical progress on this issue for years. The positive populist simply asks what system will provide the best outcomes for people at the lowest cost, without any ideological hang-ups about words like "universal" when applied to our health. We are comfortable with a guarantee that K–12 education is "universal," and paid for by the state. Why not health?

Americans might believe that those who don't work shouldn't get paid, but do Americans feel those who can't pay shouldn't get sick? Of course not. No American hospital emergency room will turn away someone who can't pay—but those very expensive emergency room costs get passed through the system, to those with private insurance and to taxpayers. So in that sense, the United States already has "universal" health coverage—it's just the most inefficient and expensive possible variant of it.

So the positive populist would agree with Democrats that we need universal coverage, but also agree with Republicans when they say that in healthcare, as in most other fields, competition and consumer choice make things better. We need radically expanded choice and competition in the delivery of healthcare so we get the benefits of the revolutionary medical innovation that competition brings. That means moving to a wide-open healthcare marketplace, not the rigged, closed system we have, where massive corporations are buying up doctors and entire hospitals and limiting choice.

But what we don't need is unlimited choice and competition in insurance. That's the part of the system where the overriding human need is for security. Even in today's allegedly free market system, consumers don't really have choice over insurance: it's an illusion for all but the top 10 percent or so who buy a private policy or pay outright. For most, control over health insurance rests with the employer, not the consumer. In the end, working Americans just want to know that they're covered, that they don't have to worry that illness and injury will result in debilitating cost. That their children will be protected come what may. That's it. End of story.

So the positive populist vision for healthcare would look very much like the vision of school choice put forward by the school reform movement: services that are paid for out of general taxation and guaranteed by the state, but competitively provided by the market in the form of for-profit or nonprofit enterprises. It's all about separating healthcare and health coverage. They are not the same, and it makes no sense to treat them the same. If we combine universal coverage with free market care, we can simultaneously meet the objectives of reformers on all sides. Conservatives can think of it as a free market voucher system for healthcare. Liberals can think of it as universal health insurance. Such a system would have the added benefit of saving taxpayers trillions of dollars and helping to reduce the fiscal deficit by eliminating the vast waste that is sucked into America's medical-industrial complex.

Of course, a key element of Positive Populism is localism: the idea that decisions should be made as close to the people affected by them as possible. In that spirit, we should acknowledge that one of the biggest defects of the current healthcare system in America is its astonishing degree of centralization—both administratively with the federal government playing such an outsize role, and operationally with the consolidation of the insurance, hospital, and pharmaceutical industries into a smaller and smaller number of giant players. A radical decentralization of the US healthcare system is long overdue, and the decoupling of health insurance and healthcare that is the positive populist way forward could help move us in that direction—either nationally, or state by state.

Government-insured *but market-delivered* at the doctor-patient level: Universal Free Market Healthcare is the future, and it's a vital part of the morally and economically savvy way to offer every American the economic security that is the essential platform for opportunity.

2. A BUSINESS-FRIENDLY LIVING WAGE

"It is a serious national evil that any class . . . should receive less than a living wage in return for their utmost exertions," argued not Bernie Sanders but rather the free market champion Winston Churchill, who supported Great Britain's first minimum wage legislation in 1909.

I agree with Churchill. If you work full-time, in return for your "utmost exertions," surely you should be able to live on what you earn, instead of having to rely on government handouts. Isn't that the very basis of human dignity—self-reliance? And shouldn't it also be the simple and basic foundation of economic security: the confidence that if you work, you'll be okay, that you can count on having the basics of a decent life? But we are a long way from that seemingly obvious and uncontroversial ideal. Economic security is elusive for millions of Americans today, men and women (rather more women, actually) who work hard—often more than one job—but can't possibly live on what they earn. That doesn't just affect them: it affects their family. Partners should be able to spend time together; parents should be able to spend time with their children. Having to work multiple jobs to make ends meet is the reality for many working Americans today, an outrageous state of affairs in the land that made "family values" famous.

Technology, of course, is making things worse. A vastly expanded set of choices for consumers, available to anyone anywhere at the click of a mouse, means that there is an unrelenting downward pressure on prices and therefore on costs. What is one of the biggest components of any company's costs? Wages.

Yes, it's true that cheaper prices are good for consumers, but they're devastating for workers' wages. And the wage slump has hit certain groups of workers particularly hard. While the overall wage statistics show a small decline over the last few decades, for those without college degrees, it has been much sharper. One study followed the earnings of high school–educated workers for two decades starting in the late 1990s. Aged 37 or 38 in 1996, they were earning an average of $44,209 a year. By their mid-50s, in 2014, they were earning $32,298—a cut of 27 percent over the course of their prime working years.

The current policy mechanism intended to address the issue of poverty pay is the minimum wage. America's federal minimum wage is $7.25 an hour and has been since 2009. That's not a problem if you're a student working a few hours a week for spending money. I remember being deliriously happy as a teenager if I managed to find a temporary work placement earning £2.80 an hour, instead of the usual £2.

But for the millions of Americans working full-time—and overtime—they can't live on the minimum wage, especially if they have children. While some states and cities mandate higher minimum wages, none of them are high enough to meet the threshold of a living wage—the amount needed to afford basic living expenses in the local area. And the bottom-line federal minimum wage is laughably inadequate, equaling $290 per 40-hour workweek, or an annual $15,080—barely enough to keep one single person living above the poverty line. Surely Americans can agree that everyone who works full-time should be nowhere near the poverty line: they should be able to live on what they earn. That's the consensus in Australia, for example, which has the world's highest minimum wage and has enjoyed remarkable economic stability compared to other countries. The generous minimum wage there is also seen to contribute to the erosion of class barriers and a more cohesive society.

Thus far, government's solution has been to top off low-wage-earning families with a confusing bureaucratic mess of welfare payments such as food stamps, housing subsidies, Medicaid, and the complex Earned Income Tax Credit. Combined, these various programs help families live above the poverty line, although the complexity and inhumanity of the system still leave many to fall through the cracks.

As if that's not bad enough, these government programs are actually a hidden subsidy to businesses, allowing them to exploit workers through poverty pay: they can get away with paying their employees less than what they need to live on, knowing that the taxpayer will pick up the tab. For example, Walmart's minimum wage employees wind up costing taxpayers $6.2 billion in public assistance, according to a 2014 report by Americans for Tax Fairness. That's a $6.2 billion subsidy to Walmart right there. The unfairness is also reflected in the way payroll taxes work: In theory, the burden of payroll tax is split between employers and employees, each paying half. In reality, the employee pays almost all of it because employers simply reduce wages by the amount of their payroll tax liability. (That's one reason why cutting payroll taxes for workers should be a much higher political priority than cutting income taxes.)

Our illogical and unjust system is not a random accident. It is the result of deliberate policy choices. It is an elitist system because it has been designed to favor employers rather than employees, the owners of businesses rather than the workers. In its crushing rejection of the values of hard work, self-reliance, and opportunity it is a complete betrayal of some of the most inspiring things America is supposed to stand for. Moreover, if you want to get partisan about it, it's also a betrayal of the free market and everything that conservatives profess to stand for: a system that subsidizes business with taxpayer money in order to force millions of hardworking, responsible Americans and their families to rely on the government for their existence. Insanity!

But wait, as they say—it gets worse. At the same time as sub-sidizing businesses by allowing them to pay workers too little and topping up the difference, government also taxes business in various ways. Walmart, for example, employs 1.5 million workers in the United States and pays billions in corporate taxes. So let's get this straight: business pays workers less than they need to live, and government makes up the difference in welfare payments. Government also takes money from business through taxation, some of which is recycled to fund the benefits that minimum wage employees need. It's a crazy merry-go-round of money and bureaucracy that keeps people dependent and government big.

The positive populist would cut through it all with two very simple, practical, pro-worker propositions: first, make sure that everyone who works full-time can live on what they earn, and second, avoid putting extra burdens on business that might cause fewer jobs to be created. There's a straightforward way to achieve this: cut out the bureaucratic welfare state middleman.

Here's the plan: require every employer to pay every full-time employee or equivalent a living wage, and cut employer taxes by the same amount. The aim should be no net impact on the employer's bottom line: all we're doing is cutting out the government middleman. Think of it as a Business-Friendly Living Wage.

This would be, as its name suggests, enough for any adult to live on. It would be significantly higher than the $7.25 federal minimum wage and calculated locally to take account of local living costs. For example, the percentage of New Yorkers living at or below the federal poverty line hovers around 20 percent—but according to the Federation of Protestant Welfare Agencies, 42 percent of New Yorkers lack the resources to meet their basic needs. A family of four needs $70,000 to be self-sufficient in the Bronx and $72,000 in Brooklyn. In the past, business leaders like Henry Ford believed it was both morally right and economically sensible to pay workers a decent wage, rather than the minimum they could get away with. Today's corporations—with a few exceptions like Costco—seem to have a different morality, hence the need for regulatory action on poverty pay.

Economists debate whether minimum wage increases prompt employers to forgo hiring either by asking existing employees to do more or turning to automation. Some studies suggest that younger workers, women, and extremely low-skilled workers who make the absolute minimum tend to suffer the most. Other evidence contradicts these claims. The Business-Friendly Living Wage circumvents this unwinnable debate by aiming for a zero net impact on business costs. Furthermore, if employers automatically deposit a portion of the higher wages they are paying into a personal retirement account for employees, rather than sending that money to the massively underfunded, unsustainable Social Security Administration, so much the better. The personalization of work-related benefits and financial products like pensions is going to be so important in a world where more people are self-employed and work itself becomes much more fragmented and episodic. Let people take charge of their own economic security. Disconnect the merry-go-round.

Similarly, the 70 percent of Americans with employer-sponsored healthcare plans might see their wages rise if Universal Free Market Healthcare is enacted. The cost of employer-provided healthcare has been creeping upward for decades. In 2016, employers' contribution to employees' healthcare ranged between 6 and 9 percent of their total compensation, according to the Bureau of Labor Statistics. Ten years ago, they ranged between 5.5 and 8 percent.

We could also experiment with variations in order to test the impact. The Business-Friendly Living Wage could in some states be something reserved for people over twenty-five or even over thirty. It might be a useful tool in combating the scourge of family breakdown, which has such a devastating effect on poverty and inequality (see Chapter 4): the living wage could be something that you get only if you are married.

This approach to the problem of low incomes is an example of how Positive Populism can reconcile competing ideological positions: it achieves the wage security Democrats favor, while taking account of Republicans' pro-business concerns. And it reduces government bureaucracy in the process.

It also goes with the grain of our shared values and social norms, unlike more radical ideas that are gaining currency. Some are ready to do away with the relationship between wages and work altogether. They see a future where there's simply no economic value to be added by the unskilled employee willing to work hard. The "universal basic income," a guaranteed welfare payment for everyone, regardless of station in life, is an extreme idea now gaining significant traction among the elitists of Silicon Valley, perhaps because they feel guilty about the negative economic outcomes of the disruption and insecurity they are causing.

Such a scheme, however, ignores the fact that doing meaningful work and being rewarded for it is a basic human need. For that most human of reasons, I believe universal basic income is a non-starter in America. Getting people "off the dole" and into the workforce has a fundamentally positive impact on their lives, and, far from decoupling work and income, we should be requiring people on public assistance to take any job available.

Peter Cove, the CEO of America Works, is among those with the clearest vision of how harmful a universal basic income would be. Cove joined the War on Poverty in 1965 as a New York City federal grant administrator, and that experience changed his viewpoint about paying people not to work:

I saw with my own eyes the value of work—any kind of paid work—in reducing welfare dependency and attacking poverty. I learned that if we helped welfare clients get jobs, even entry-level jobs, they would then attend to their other needs. By contrast, if the government gave them money and other benefits, they were likely to remain dependent.

Americans' extremely generous War on Poverty began in 1964—yet more than fifty years later, the poverty rate has fallen by only a few points, to 15 percent of the population. Along the way, bureaucratic welfare rules and administrators created the counterproductive incentives for families living below the poverty line that harmed those families as well as the taxpayers subsidizing them.

But the official poverty rate doesn't come close to fully capturing the experience of the working poor. Since the 1970s, at least half—and maybe two-thirds—of Americans, despite growth in the economy overall, have been at best treading water. The positive populist recognizes the upsides of trade, technology, and (well-regulated) immigration but cannot simply shrug off the persistence and pain of wage stagnation. What economic growth the country has experienced has not been widely enjoyed, and fair pay is the least the winners can do for the left-behind Americans who are willing to work. It is evident that incremental fixes have failed to tackle this problem: that's why it's time for a revolutionary approach, and the Business-Friendly Living Wage is an example of one that we should all be able to get behind.

3. HOME OWNERSHIP FOR ALL:
GREEN/BROWN ZONING

Your healthcare, your income—for those Americans living in economic insecurity, there's one more vital piece of the jigsaw: housing. Whether it's paying the rent or mortgage, the cost, stress, and time involved in commuting from somewhere affordable to a job with a living wage, or just the basic nightmare of having to settle for living someplace (or with people) you really don't like because it's all you can pay for . . . housing is one of the biggest causes of anxiety for working Americans. Whether you're a young person starting out or a working family trying not to live hours away from opportunity, housing is too much of a challenge, especially near economically thriving cities that have priced out all but the most successful.

There's a simple reason: housing is too expensive. There's a simple reason for that, too. Just as our approach to wages and incomes is designed to serve the needs of the comfortable and wealthy (the owners of businesses rather than the workers), housing policy is typically designed to cater to the needs of those who already own property rather than those who aspire to.

This elitism, often gussied up in progressive-sounding goals like environmentalism, contributes to a shortage of housing supply, which of course increases the price. But it's not just about the so-called NIMBYs blocking development; there is a structural elitism as well. You see it in the way that big developers, corruptly in bed with state and local politicians, hoard land and rig the rules to block competition from independent home builders. You see it in the way that housing policy is designed with the cultural elite in mind rather than regular working-class families who want detached homes with gardens rather than a cramped apartment in an up-and-coming city neighborhood. And you see it most clearly in the tax code.

One of the most unfair aspects of the American tax code is the deduction available for home mortgage interest. Given the insecurity working-class people face over housing—whether they can afford a down payment and qualify for a mortgage, what will happen if interest rates rise, how they will afford maintenance—this deduction does nothing but help rich people afford slightly pricier homes—and help inflate property prices to begin with. Those it benefits the most are people who can afford million-dollar mortgages and $100,000 home equity loans. But large real estate developers and agencies—with deep pockets and lobbyists in Washington—love this deduction because it incentivizes people to buy bigger and more expensive homes.

Where are the incentives to build smaller, more affordable homes for working people who rent but would like to own? One of Margaret Thatcher's greatest triumphs as prime minister was her "Right to Buy" initiative to help those in public housing purchase their home from the local council. It was a transfer of assets, a spreading of wealth, on an epic scale: housing policy that was truly populist, and which led to greater economic security for millions. We need a similarly ambitious populist housing revolution in America today.

Zoning policies need to change. Part of that involves allowing construction projects that would increase density or potentially exert downward pressure on the average home price in any given neighborhood. But taking on NIMBYism is not a silver bullet. For a start, it's important to recognize that the NIMBYs are not just millionaires in mansions: they also include working families with legitimate concerns about their quality of life. Ask residents what scale and style would be acceptable to them; don't just award a contract to a cronyist developer who doesn't care about the current occupants of a neighborhood.

In any case, more dense urban development is often more costly and produces expensive high-end housing that doesn't bring home ownership within the reach of the people who really need it. A true housing revolution would mean taking on not just the NIMBYs but also the urban policy elitists who argue against construction on urban fringes because of their prejudice against what they snootily refer to as "suburban sprawl." Instead their vision is to warehouse their beloved "knowledge workers" in high-rise hipster hutches: without kitchens (because "everyone" uses food delivery apps), without parking (because "everyone" uses ride-sharing apps), and of course without yards (because Instagramming a plant is so much easier than actually growing one).

This is not how most people want to live. Most people want to live in a regular family home with some outside space. We can give them that opportunity if we open up space for construction: on the edges of urban areas but right in the center, too. As online shopping replaces consumer demand for shopping malls, rezone those areas for housing. As self-driving cars reduce the need for parking garages, rezone them. And bring down the cost of construction—and therefore the price of home ownership—by sweeping away archaic rules and restrictions such as many states' laws banning nonunion labor for any construction project.

The positive populist understands that an ownership society is a major driver of economic security and community life. But the focus has to be on policies that support the working poor instead of million-dollar-home owners doing high-end renovations with their equity lines of credit.

Zoning laws and regulations are more often than not a gift to big developers and a recipe for corruption and abuse. The complexity of the system favors insiders and discriminates against working people; the only ones who really benefit are the developers, and the bureaucrats and politicians they have in their pocket. This policy mess is the reason housing costs so much and home ownership has become so elusive for so many.

Why are we allowing politicians and bureaucrats to micromanage what gets built, and where? Imagine if we applied the same thinking to other parts of the economy: if politicians and bureaucrats had to approve the design of new consumer products before they were launched or if they could intervene in the development process for new software. Everything would grind to a halt—just like the supply of housing has.

We have to remove arbitrary top-down control of housing and replace it with a simple, understandable, populist alternative. No more tinkering with zoning rules and incentives and subsidies for low-cost affordable housing. It hasn't worked. In fact, it makes things worse.

Instead, we should implement a simple designation: every piece of land is allocated either for development or for nature. If it's allocated for development, then whoever owns the land can build whatever they want. If it's allocated for nature, no one can build anything. That's it. That's the system. Let's call it Green/Brown Zoning.

Yes, of course, I can hear the objections: How can you just let anything get built? We'll have eyesores all over the place. Neighborhoods will be ruined! As if that doesn't happen now. The truth is, overwhelmingly, *if you trust people and give them responsibility, they will behave responsibly*—just look at the neighborhood planning story in Chapter 7. Green/Brown Zoning will also mean much more land set aside for conservation, which will be available for anyone to enjoy. Freedom doesn't lead to perfection, but it's better than the alternative. Let's take power over what gets built out of the hands of the elite and put it in the hands of the people. That's the positive populist way to solve our housing crisis and at last help working people achieve that critical part of economic security: owning your own home.

OF COURSE, UNDERPINNING THESE three big ideas for reform is the ongoing need for economic dynamism. The Populist Economy needs to be a fast-growing economy. As we've already seen, when it comes to the daily reality for those in the lower half of the income scale, a rising tide does not lift all boats. That's why this chapter has focused on specific targeted reforms to address the specific, persistent manifestations of economic insecurity—problems that have hurt working people in good economic times and bad. But there's no question that faster economic growth makes it easier to raise living standards across the board.

So the positive populist economic agenda must also include policies that will help increase economic growth rather than harm it. While rising GDP by itself has not been enough to help the working poor, as the past four decades have shown, stagnant GDP will hurt the working poor more than any other group: it's their jobs that are typically the first to vanish in an economic slump.

For example, Barack Obama was the first president in American history not to have a single year of growth above 3 percent. The annual average during his administration was an anemic 1.8 percent—well below the post–World War II average of 2.7 percent. While this stagnation hurt most working- and middle-class people, it is an especially sad irony that during this period, incomes fell more for black people than any other racial or ethnic group.

What does a populist pro-growth strategy look like? First, you've got to boost the productivity of the economy: how much is produced with any given amount of input. As we've already seen, rising productivity does not automatically translate into higher incomes for working people: not by a long shot. But without rising productivity, you've got absolutely no chance. The most important factor in productivity growth is infrastructure: transportation, energy, digital infrastructure all need a massive upgrade in America. This is one of the rare issues that most politicians seem to agree on, so let's hope they make it happen.

The second vital factor for growth is deregulation. Promises to "cut red tape" have become a political cliché over the years but that doesn't make it any less of a priority. It seems to have been the one thing that President Trump's administration implemented effectively from day one, and the results were quickly apparent in the form of increased business confidence and investment. But government has an inbuilt tendency to grow and regulate—much of it, let's face it, aided and abetted by a combination of public opinion ("something must be done") and concerted lobbying by insiders and Big Business. After all, one of the best ways for an incumbent business to protect its position is to force upstart competitors to have to comply with costly regulations. So there must be constant vigilance and determination in the battle to hold back the regulatory state. That's not just a job for politicians, but for the judicial branch, too—there has been a creeping usurpation of power from the legislature to unaccountable bureaucrats in the administrative state, and it is often only the careful application of the law that can prevent their regulatory overreach.

The third core component of a populist economic growth plan is the one that may seem the most counterintuitive. A dynamic economy is essential if we're going to create decent-paying jobs for American workers, and that depends on businesses' ability to be competitive. The corporate tax regime for American companies was for a long time a real barrier to that. Keeping business taxes low is not only in the interests of those who own businesses: it's in the interests of workers, too. It may not translate into higher wages (contrary to the claims of many politicians), but it will spur investment—both domestically and from overseas—which will lead to more jobs being created in the first place. The dramatic 2017 corporate tax cut was a step in the right direction: but it still left America with a corporate tax rate higher than many competitors'. We should be the lowest.

If we implement pro-growth policies along these lines and combine them with the specific ideas put forward here to address the root causes of economic security—Universal Free Market Healthcare, a Business-Friendly Living Wage, and Green/Brown Zoning—then we can start to turn around the terrible stagnation that has afflicted so many working families in America for so long. But we should not be satisfied with such remedial action. The populist economy demands more.

When my parents emigrated from Hungary to England in the 1950s, nearly half of Britons worked in manufacturing. It was a place where hardworking but unskilled laborers could put in an honest day's work and build an economically secure life for themselves and their families, climbing the ladder of opportunity. Social mobility and upward progress was the reality for most. But today, only around one in ten people work in manufacturing, and the promise of a steady job leading to progress through life—and then for the next generation—seems to have all but vanished.

We need to prepare people for success in the industries and jobs of the future, and that means building on the foundations of economic security to provide working people with real opportunity.

IN A NUTSHELL . . .

At least half of all Americans live in economic insecurity. That is a deliberate policy choice, and we can change it. We must choose a secure, pro-worker policy agenda as the foundation of the Populist Economy.

1. **Reduce the burden of healthcare on people and business:** Healthcare costs are the main driver of economic insecurity for working Americans. Universal Free Market Health Care—government backed, competitively provided by the market—is the best way to remove the incredible stress healthcare causes while ensuring it is provided with maximum quality and innovation, at lowest possible cost.

2. **A Business-Friendly Living Wage:** If you work full-time you should be able to live on what you earn. Make the minimum wage a living wage and make sure it's affordable by cutting payroll taxes by the amount of the wage increase. In the process eliminate the need for government bureaucracy to top up low pay with subsidies and welfare.

3. **Green/Brown Zoning:** Home ownership is the bedrock for the American middle class but increasingly unattainable as the property-owning elite block new housing. Put the needs of working people first and cut the costs of housebuilding. Abolish all current zoning regulation and replace with a simple alternative: Green/Brown Zoning, where land is designated either for nature or development; if the latter, anything can be built by whoever owns the land.

2

OPPORTUNITY

NO MATTER WHERE you grew up—Hungary, like my parents, or Britain, like me—you heard America called the "Land of Opportunity." For anyone with ambition and the determination to work hard, America's streets were paved with gold. Start at the bottom; work your way up; own your own home; retire comfortably in your sixties.

Now that I live in the United States, I feel incredibly lucky to be here. My wife and I moved from London to the beautiful Bay Area in 2012. She had been leading Google's global communications and government relations, but doing that high-pressure job from London. When Sonny, our second son, was born, the travel and time difference became too much: I left my job at 10 Downing Street and we moved to California. At first teaching at Stanford I then soon decided to take the plunge and start a business of my own. I can barely believe that five years after moving here, I have been the CEO of a tech company and the host of a TV show, and have published a couple of books. What an incredible opportunity this country has given me.

But the truth is that all too often these days in America, those "streets paved with gold" are accessible only to those who—like us—arrived well-off and well connected.

If you've got an entry-level job in Silicon Valley, some student loan debt, and no family trust fund, perhaps you live in a truck parked on a tech company's campus, a large box in someone's living room, or a garage—all real-life living arrangements featured on the *San Francisco Chronicle*'s website. If you're a janitor or cafeteria worker in Silicon Valley, perhaps you face a two- or even three-hour commute before you find a neighborhood where the cost of housing approaches affordability. It's not exactly the American Dream, is it?

Once the basic foundation of economic security has been provided, people need to be at least relatively confident that talent and effort do not go unrewarded. Happiness, of course, can never be guaranteed. But the right to *pursue* happiness must be. That is the American Dream, and its conditions must be restored. Opportunity for all, not just the elite, is an essential part of the Populist Economy.

By 2018, two-thirds of all jobs in the United States will require more than a high school diploma, according to the Georgetown Center for Education and the Workforce. Yet funneling all high school graduates into universities isn't going to increase their opportunities. As it is, 40 percent of college graduates lack the reasoning skills to manage white-collar work, a 2014 study by the Council for Aid to Education (part of the RAND Corporation) found. What opportunities await that 40 percent, especially if they carry the US average student loan debt of $37,000?

If you don't have an inside track somehow, it's hard to find a permanent position these days. In 2017, slightly more than 40 percent of American employers told the Manpower Group they can't find qualified people to fill the jobs they have available—the highest talent shortage in ten years. So rather than grant opportunities to new employees, they have doubled their rates of internal promotion. Across the country, you hear stories of employers bemoaning the fact that they can't find qualified workers with the skills they need who can pass a drug test. What is going so wrong?

Both Democrats and Republicans have presided over decades of flat wages, a housing market that is increasingly difficult to enter, and forced early retirements. We need a policy revolution that focuses on the root cause of all these problems. And it starts by looking inward.

Since the modern "globalist" ideology began to be implemented by the elites in the late 1980s and early '90s, much of the populist rhetoric around jobs, incomes, and opportunity has been focused on trade and immigration. "'We're being ripped off by the Mexicans and the Chinese" or "We're importing so much cheap labor that it's leaving American workers on the scrap heap" are the common refrains. Well, yes, we are being ripped off by the elitist obsession with free trade, and I'm all for better, fairer trade deals—especially a much tougher stance against China. (You can read about that in Chapter 6.) And yes, it's true that uncontrolled immigration has had serious negative consequences for American workers in terms of lost jobs and lower wages.

But trade and immigration are not the whole story when it comes to opportunity for working Americans. The biggest factor contributing to the economic and social pain of the last few decades is in fact increased automation and technology, which make it increasingly difficult for employers to justify paying people wages to do what machines can do better, faster, and cheaper. We are in the middle—some would say at the start—of a major economic transition, and the elites have not prepared for this moment. They have blithely embraced the tech-enabled future without paying attention to the real human toll on the victims of this cold-eyed disruption: working Americans whose jobs, livelihoods, and communities are being automated away.

One of the reasons for that is the geographical distribution of the disruption. Just as we've seen a concentration of power in the economy—big corporations getting bigger—we've seen a concentration of growth—big cities booming while other parts of the country are left to decay.

We desperately need a response to this wrenching transition that doesn't just rail at the changes—although frankly there's nothing wrong with a bit of that, given the heartless behavior of our elitist overlords—but actually (and urgently) puts in place positive steps to help working people move happily from the old economy to the new. We also have to make sure that we don't repeat the mistakes of the past and add to the problem we already have.

So much has been written about this topic, but so little of it puts forward anything other than bland generalities about improving education and training "to meet the needs of the twenty-first-century workplace." Well yes! But how?

The truth is, the problem is structural. It's not about a few more new courses here and there. A bit more money for community colleges. That's totally inadequate. Instead we have to rethink the whole structure of education, and redesign it around the central asset that will determine whether or not people can flourish in this new economy.

That asset is the productive capacity of American citizens of all ages, either to work with automation and technology, or in those more human areas where the machines will struggle to compete and displace. So how do we increase human productivity in the United States? There are three big ideas set out in this chapter. We need a transformation in our school system and we need an even bigger change in how we think about training and education beyond school. At the same time, we can't ignore the impact of immigration on our economy: sensible, controlled immigration can enhance opportunity and the productivity of working Americans; the broken system we have today does the opposite.

1. RADICAL SCHOOL REFORM

One of the greatest tragedies in the world is the inequality of opportunity for the multitude of bright children who never get a chance at a decent education.

Many of the opportunities available to me are the direct result of a radical educational intervention that changed my personal trajectory. Though my Hungarian relatives had been doctors and teachers, my own status as the son of immigrants who had arrived in the UK with nothing was a bit more precarious.

When I was a boy in the 1970s, Great Britain was in a socialism-fueled tailspin. The resulting financial crisis was so dire the country's Labour government was forced to apply to the International Monetary Fund for a $4 billion loan. My struggling father returned to Hungary when I was four, and my mother and I lived in a dingy basement apartment in Brighton until she met my stepfather, a construction worker.

Fortunately for me, Brighton is a short drive to the Horsham campus of Christ's Hospital, the remarkable and unique independent school that would change my life. Originally founded in 1552 through King Edward VI's appeal to private benefactors in the City of London, Christ's Hospital's mission was to provide food, clothing, lodging, and "a little learning for fatherless children and other poor men's children" so they were properly trained to assume positions in commerce or trade by the age of fifteen.

Today students from all walks of life attend, most of them for free, paid for through the school's charitable foundation. For the 20 percent or so who do pay, fees are assessed according to family income. A visitor will see children of every race and mostly disadvantaged backgrounds wearing the distinctive Tudor-style uniform, a tradition as old as the school itself. "Christ's Hospital has pioneered social mobility and challenged social inequality to provide an unrivaled start in life for disadvantaged children for nearly five centuries," and its mission is to "offer . . . an education of such breadth and excellence as will fit them pre-eminently for work and service in society . . . and enable them to compete with their peers for opportunities in further education and careers."

The unique education I received at Christ's Hospital put me on the path to an Oxford University degree and then to the heart of politics and government in Westminster. I owe pretty much everything to that school and still vividly recall the solemn and emotional leaving service in the school's magnificent chapel at the end of which the head teacher delivers "the Charge" to the pupils who are about to head out into the world: "I charge you never to forget the great benefits that you have received in this place, and in time to come, according to your means, to do all that you can to enable others to enjoy the same advantage."

Well, I haven't forgotten, and one way or another I have worked throughout my career to deliver that charge. (Another thing I haven't forgotten: a stinging rebuke that instilled in me the value of persistence. To this day I can see the handwritten end-of-term report from one of my teachers after I had defiantly handed in a blank sheet of paper instead of attempting an assignment I felt was beyond my ability: *A little less self-pity and a little more determination would work wonders."* Indeed. Ever since then I've come to realize that the most important factor for success in any field is to just get on with it and keep going.)

Christ's Hospital was founded in the sixteenth century and transformed my opportunities in twentieth-century Britain. It gave me, for free, the kind of education that elsewhere only money can buy. Now, in the twenty-first-century United States, we need to completely rethink education so that every child has that opportunity. Why? First, because we're seeing that social mobility in America has basically stalled. Those at the top are entrenching their advantages and everyone else is increasingly stuck. Education used to be the ladder of opportunity but today that ladder is very badly broken. The second reason for revolutionary change in education is that the transformation we're seeing in our economy is set to dramatically sharpen the divide between the well educated and everyone else. The stories we read on an almost daily basis: that "the robots are coming after your job," that artificial intelligence and other forms of technology will wipe out whole professions, destroying not just (or not even mainly) manual jobs but white-collar jobs, too, the kind that so many have aspired to over the ages—doctors, lawyers, accountants . . . these stories may be presented a little too breathlessly on occasion but they are not qualitatively wrong.

The elite casually throw around phrases like "there's no such thing as a job for life anymore," or "people will just have to learn new skills if their jobs disappear." They rarely stop to think about the emotional and psychological hurt caused by those on the receiving end of such advice from on high. But the fundamental premise is true: the changes that technology is bringing about in our economy means that traditional education will be almost completely inadequate to prepare people to thrive and prosper. We used to think of education as the essence of opportunity. Unless we radically reshape it, education will become opportunity's enemy: imprisoning people with useless knowledge and out-of-date tools.

To navigate the unpredictable future economy successfully, children today need a highly individualized, custom-fit education, one where the central aim is not the teaching of content but the forming of character, in particular a proficiency in self-directed learning, since that will become essential through life. This is miles away from the kind of education delivered by the nineteenth-century factory model that typifies our government schools today. The Industrial Revolution has long been supplanted by the Technology Revolution, yet education has remained structurally the same.

American public schools began in the 1820s, when a docile, obedient workforce was needed to fill the Industrial Revolution's factories. Students learned by rote memorization, sat in neatly ordered rows, and competed for hierarchical standing. In the late 1800s, the US commissioner of education William T. Harris praised big "modern" schools for having "the appearance of a machine," in fostering "regularity, punctuality, silence, and conformity to order."

That approach is a disaster today, especially for children in poor and working-class families. In 2014, America's high school graduate rate was at a modern record of 83.2 percent, according to the America's Promise Alliance, but students from low-income families lag 14 points behind everyone else. Why would we expect factory schools to reach these children any better than government-run poverty programs reach their families? In any case, factory schools aren't the right way to educate even the most privileged children.

In 2016, the *San Jose Mercury News* published a telling letter from Marc Vincenti, a former English teacher in my nearby community of Palo Alto: "[W]e ought to be fixing our high schools,

which countenance misery-inducing cheating, classes as unhealth-
ily overcrowded as our local jails, relentless grade-reporting, all-
day student access to social media, and homework and AP loads
that lead to massive sleep-deprivation."

Mr. Vincenti wrote because Palo Alto's suicide rate is 14.1 per
100,000 among youth between the ages of 10 and 24. Nationally
among the same age group, the rate is 5.4 per 100,000. (Interest-
ingly, Palo Alto's poverty rate is one-third of the national poverty rate.) What does that say about the "successful" products of
wealthy Palo Alto's factory school system?

Students don't need to be passive receptacles of knowledge,
constantly tested and weighed against their peers until they feel
worthless (and sleep-deprived) enough to kill themselves. It's
a waste of their potential, failing to encourage innate curiosity.
They need to be self-directed seekers of knowledge and able to
apply what they learn with minimal oversight. By their very nature, government-run institutions with their layers of bureaucracy
and centrally directed conformity are incapable of such a vision.
Standardized testing has been the be-all and end-all in American
schools for years, costing billions of dollars, and it's worse than
useless.

But both Republicans and Democrats cling to the factory
system they know. Republicans are drawn to its disciplined pro-
gression and objective testing; Democrats are drawn to the egali-
tarianism promised to students and job security promised to
teachers. Conservatives have promoted "school choice," but charter schools—public schools somewhat freed from government
bureaucracy—are only a small step in the right direction, despite
the fact that they generally perform well. At least they weaken the
grip of teachers' unions, which protect professional mediocrity at
the expense of students. But charter schools don't represent nearly
enough of a break with the past, and don't reach nearly enough

children. The answer isn't just a few more educational options to supplement a failing system.

The twin challenges of the collapse in social mobility and the transformation in the economy demand a complete rethink. That's already happening in a few small pockets of educational innovation, many of them close to where I live in Silicon Valley.

For example, the Khan Lab School, where our two children go and where we were among the founder parents, is entirely focused on helping children become enthusiastic independent learners. Children are grouped by "independence level" rather than traditional grade or age; they progress through disciplines on the basis of mastering a task. If it takes one child two weeks, they move up to the next task then and there; if it takes a child in the same class a year, well, that's how long they will spend on it. Each pupil sets their own learning plan, with self-described goals that are evaluated together with teachers on a regular basis. The school focuses on teaching practical skills of teamwork, creativity, and entrepreneurialism as much as academic content.

You may say: well, that's fine for the fancy folks of the Silicon Valley tech elite—try doing that throughout the public school system. And that's exactly the point: right now, the really transformative education innovation is being enjoyed mainly by the privileged few. To help reboot social mobility, and to help every child in every part of the country prepare for the unpredictable twenty-first-century economy, we need to democratize educational innovation. We can do that by allowing individuals, groups of parents, nonprofits, social enterprises, for-profit companies—whoever is committed to bringing new ways of teaching and learning—to start new schools and offer a new education to children of all backgrounds, everywhere.

That is the positive populist answer to factory schools and the threat they pose to equal opportunity: tear down the failing system and replace it with an open, parent-powered marketplace. The state monopoly on education must be ended. The apparatus of government control has failed working Americans and their children for decades, and must be abolished—from the Education Department in Washington, DC, to state capitals to school boards. There is no reason for a teacher to be a government employee—whether on the federal, state, or local level. Today, private schools can hire teachers using their best judgment—offering competitive salaries from the start, instead of costly retirement pensions that incentivize burned-out teachers to become "lifers" in the system. Private schools can also fire teachers if their performance—which can be judged by parental and student feedback—is found lacking. Why should that degree of accountability be reserved for the rich?

We need a nationally funded school voucher system, whereby the federal government guarantees funding for every student but independent organizations like Christ's Hospital or Khan Lab School provide the education, which will come in all shapes and sizes of school. Whether they are for-profit or nonprofit, these organizations would be directly accountable to parents. But we need to make sure that all children—no matter how wealthy or impoverished their families are—have access to the same amount of money for education, at a cost-of-living-adjusted level set by the federal government. Liberals are correct when they criticize the disparities in school funding: rich communities fund their schools with donations and property taxes based on their enormous real estate wealth, whereas poor schools are dependent on a pittance collected from volunteer bake sales.

Elitists will immediately condemn this plan by claiming that you can't possibly expect parents to bear the burden of educational responsibility in such a universal free market system (translation: "poor parents can't be trusted to make wise choices for their kids"). What patronizing nonsense. While serving in government I visited one of the largest and poorest slums in the world, in Lagos, Nigeria, and witnessed the inspiring sight of parents rejecting a free, failing government school and instead sending their children to a private school established by a local social entrepreneur, charging a few dollars in fees. The phenomenon of "private schools for the poor," based on the power of parental choice, is sweeping the world from Africa to India and beyond. It is exposing the failure of elitist education policy and the determination of parents to secure opportunity for their children. How dare anyone say that can't work in America?

Public policy can't determine whether a child is born into a rich family or a poor one, but it can ensure that all children get the best possible education, no matter where they live or how much money their family has. Universal Free Market Education, with its open, innovative spirit and commitment to equalizing opportunity, could be the catalyst for a much wider range of schools to prepare the next, highly diverse generation of Americans.

2. UNIVERSAL FREE MARKET TRAINING

Universal Free Market Education would be a big change. But when it comes to education beyond school, we need an even bigger one. The debate on the future of work swings from doomsday gloom—"artificial intelligence will destroy most of the jobs in the economy so we'd better get used to a life of leisure, subsisting on Universal Basic Income—just until the apocalyptic 'Singularity' happens and the intelligent machines become smarter than humans and completely take over"—to perky nonchalance: "yes, this is a change in the economy, but we've had these big transitions before—at the turn of the century half of America worked on the fields in an agrarian economy; after the Industrial Revolution only a handful work in agriculture but people still work—new jobs will be created to replace the old ones. Relax!"

One strain of populism essentially endorses the apocalyptic prediction but its main response is to rail against the Silicon Valley elites who are busy bringing about that dystopian future. The positive populist, on the other hand, tends to embrace the more optimistic scenario, but with a crucial caveat: we must absolutely not "relax." Yes, it's possible to envisage a future where new jobs are created and working Americans are equipped to take them—but we need a gargantuan rethink of policy on skills and training in order to bring that about, and people will be left behind if we leave them to navigate the fast-changing world of work on their own.

Why is that? Why can't we just leave it to people's sense of responsibility to train for their future employability? Why can't we leave it to employers? The first problem is that most working people simply can't afford to retrain. They're too busy struggling for economic survival to take a few months or even a few weeks off to learn a new skill. That's especially true when they have a family to provide for. And it's increasingly not in an employer's commercial interests to train people, either. When you can count on an employee being with your business for years, it might be worth your while spending money on their training. But people change jobs far more frequently than they used to, so an employer will find it harder to recoup investment in training. Furthermore, the rapid rise of self-employment and people hopping around from one type of work to another in the tech-driven "gig" economy makes the whole notion of an employer investing in their employee's skills outdated as a go-to model.

Solving this problem is crucial. The only way to ensure that everyone can enjoy rising income throughout the course of life is by continually increasing their personal productive capacity. That way, they will be able to keep increasing their income through their own entrepreneurialism, or if employed, it will make economic sense for employers to keep paying them more. So a populist blue-collar jobs agenda would emphasize lifelong training and vocational education. That is easy to say, but hard to do. We are already seeing how difficult it is to retrain people whose manufacturing jobs disappeared as a result of globalization and technology. Some of the skills associated with jobs that are in decline can be repurposed, but certainly not all. Increasingly, however, clerical, administrative, and professional classes—including doctors and lawyers—will need to retrain and switch careers, too. (One optimistic thought: if we faithfully implement the educational reforms outlined elsewhere in this chapter, young people in the future won't need to be "retrained" because they will embark on their working life already equipped with the mind-set and skills to pursue opportunity in many different ways.)

But in terms of the training challenge today, we are nowhere near the right answer on this, mainly because politicians (of left and right) have tended to tinker with policy in this area rather than look for revolutionary change. After the Great Recession of 2008, Washington aimed a fire hose of money at federal employment and training programs, yet by 2011, a Government Accountability Office report admitted, "little is known about the effectiveness of most programs. In fiscal year 2009, 9 federal agencies spent approximately $18 billion to administer 47 programs—an increase of 3 programs and roughly $5 billion since our 2003 report." In July 2014, Congress passed a bipartisan bill aimed at matching these expensive government training programs with the real needs of employers—and an NPR.org headline summed up the pathetic state of affairs nicely: "Congress and Biden Aim for Job Training That Actually Leads to Jobs." Too little, too late.

Other countries do this so much better. In Germany, the government pays 25 percent of employers' costs for apprentices, who receive certification when they have completed their course. Germany's unemployment rate for non-college-bound young adults is half that of the United States', where only 10 percent of Americans between the ages of eighteen and twenty-two receive on-the-job training. The Danes have an even better model—at the moment the best in the world. They don't focus on job security, but on life-long employment security. Unlike many other European countries, they have relaxed laws about hiring and firing employees, and as a result one-quarter of workers change jobs every year in the Danish private sector. Anticipating the transitions, the Danish government's "Flexicurity" system pays workers up to 90 percent of a low-wage salary while they are acquiring new training certificates and part-time degrees. Denmark has one of the lowest inequality rates in the world (and is also the happiest country in the world, according to the United Nations).

Of course, comparing Denmark to the United States is not an apples-to-apples undertaking. You see the difference not just in size and political culture but in deeper and darker ways, too, especially when you understand the connection between race and economic opportunity. The institutionalized racism that continued for a century after the end of slavery, right through America's civil rights era, is evident in the contrasting levels of employment and skill today. Only 10 percent of white Americans are classified as "low-skilled," whereas 35 percent of black Americans are in that category, according to the OECD report "Time for the United States to Reskill?"

The American ethnic group with the highest proportion of "low-skilled" workers is Hispanics, at 43 percent. "Non-English-speaking immigrants in the United States with low-educated parents are 10 times more likely to have low literacy skills . . . than native born adults whose parents have at least a high school education." Before the technological revolution, a person struggling with English could still get by. My own mother worked as a shoe store clerk to support us—until her language skills improved enough for her to join a local office's typing pool. That was then. Today computers have eliminated the need for typing pools and Zappos has ushered many a shoe store clerk into early retirement.

But these realities should not deter us from pursuing something closer to the Danish model. In part, a lot more investment will be needed. We are fooling ourselves, however, if we believe that investing more money in our current skills and training system will even come close to turning this around. The adult education and training infrastructure we have in this country is not up to the scale of economic transition that is already hitting us and will intensify. Fortunately, the source of many of these problems is also the source of potential solutions. Some of the most far-reaching innovations in Silicon Valley are all about rethinking how skills training can be designed and delivered at a fraction of the previous cost and in a way that is more effective. Start-ups like Udacity (disclosure: it was founded by a friend of mine and my wife is on the board) are pioneering online skills training and certification that can be accessed on your phone and in a way that fits with your life. Udacity's "nanodegrees" are designed in partnership with leading employers like AT&T and Google. You can complete a course, via your phone, in a matter of weeks, and be certified as trained for a completely new job. We're also seeing new alternatives to college that focus on skills that will actually be useful: the start-up Praxis, for example, takes its clients through a general work-skills boot camp before placing them in apprenticeships that lead to employment. If we can combine that kind of innovation with more state and local apprenticeships and a simple skills certification system that is recognized nationwide, that would be huge progress.

The positive populist plan for a radical overhaul of job training would open up these kinds of opportunities to everyone. What we need looks similar to the model for populist education and health reform: the up-front costs of skills training should, where necessary, be guaranteed by the state, but the training itself should be competitively provided by the market through for-profit or non-profit enterprises. That should also include money for setting up colleges in the places that have been left behind by globalization and technology: there's no reason why the "knowledge economy" can exist only in places like New York and San Francisco. With advances like 3D printing we can also imagine depressed regions revitalized by modern manufacturing. But all of these positive outcomes depend on people having the skills to pursue new opportunities. So let's put the money that government wastes on failing training programs directly in people's hands to spend on training that suits them.

3. OPPORTUNITY IMMIGRATION

We've seen that some strains of populism are too pessimistic about our ability to turn the technology revolution into opportunity for working Americans, not just the elite. The same goes for one of the other big issues for populists—perhaps the defining issue—and that's immigration.

Populists are correct to prioritize it. Put aside the accurate but policy-lite slogans about America being a "nation of immigrants": yes, obviously that's true, but it doesn't mean it's right to suspend any kind of judgment about the nature or scale of immigration that's in America's national interest at any given time. Put aside also the impact of immigration on our culture and social cohesion: we'll get to that in Chapter 6. Let's focus here on the economic aspects of immigration and in particular the role it plays in promoting opportunity: for immigrants, of course, but for Americans already here, too.

Let me start by saying that I am proudly pro-immigration: I'm an immigrant twice over—my parents were welcomed to the United Kingdom from communist Hungary and now here I am in America. I've been given opportunities beyond anything I could have imagined had I been born, raised, and stayed in the small town of Szeged in southern Hungary where most of my family still lives today. I hope I'm repaying the hospitality by making a contribution: I've started a business and am adding what I can to the national debate. But more broadly, I'm pro-immigration because it is transparently the case that immigration has created opportunity in America—not just for immigrants ourselves, but actually on a far bigger scale for Americans already here. Immigration helped America ascend the heights of global innovation and world economic dominance. Just in the recent past, immigrants have played a founding role in more than half of America's billion-dollar start-ups.

But in recent years, that positive contribution to opportunity has become obscured by an immigration experience that is very different from what we have seen in the past. Today the elite orthodoxy has shifted from being—rightly—open to immigration, to one that is for open borders. Any effort to control or restrict immigration of any kind is viewed as bigoted, racist, and un-American. This is a terrible distortion of our traditions. Open-border advocates like to cite the stirring poem on the Statue of Liberty in defense of the view that America should be open to literally anyone who wants to come here: "Bring me your tired, your poor, your huddled masses yearning to breathe free." That was—and is—a beautiful encapsulation of the spirit of America rather than a policy; still less one that's suitable for the twenty-first century. It was written in an age where for most immigrants getting to America involved an arduous weeks-long journey. Today we live in a world of cheap global air travel and technology, which means that anyone in the world can see what life is like anywhere else in the world. Do you think those two factors might have increased pretty dramatically the number of people who might consider moving to America, compared to the 1850s? And do you think we might want to have a view on that, rather than just saying, "Sure, anyone who wants to should be able to come here—that's what America is all about!"

Perhaps no politician is more clear-eyed about uncontrolled immigration's real impact on economic opportunity than left-wing populist Bernie Sanders, who chided the naïveté of "open borders" in a 2015 Vox interview with Ezra Klein: "That's a right-wing proposal, which says essentially there is no United States." Senator Sanders continued: "You know what youth unemployment is in the United States of America today? If you're a white high school graduate, it's 33 percent, Hispanic 36 percent, African American 51 percent. You think we should open the borders and bring in a lot of low-wage workers, or do you think maybe we should try to get jobs for those kids?"

Of the 36 million adults in the United States who are "low-skilled," an OECD report found, one-third are immigrants. It's understandable that Americans today—who are known around the world for their generosity—are gravely concerned about the number and kind of immigrants seeking admission to the United States. Nineteen percent of the world's immigrants arrive in America, almost twice as many as accepted by Germany and Russia combined (the second and third most common immigration destinations).

Proponents of open borders argue that Americans—young or old—don't want the jobs that unskilled immigrants are taking. Really? The evidence says something quite different: the two industries most associated with immigrant labor—farming and construction—have the highest unemployment rates among natives. Thirty-six percent of jobs in the farming, fishing, and forestry industry are filled by immigrants—and 11.9 percent of Americans in that industry are unemployed. Twenty-four percent of construction and extraction industry jobs are filled by immigrants, and the US-born unemployment rate in that field is 12.7 percent. On the other hand, industries with low unemployment rates for native-born Americans have the lowest percentage of immigrant labor. Only 11 percent of the arts, entertainment, and media industry are immigrants, and only 5.9 percent of native-born Americans in that field are unemployed. In the legal profession, 7 percent are immigrants—and only 2.7 percent of native-born lawyers report being unemployed. No wonder the elites are not concerned about open borders—they don't experience the problem firsthand. A very elite 0.4 percent of America's general population are lawyers—but 42 percent of the House of Representatives are, and 59 percent of the Senate!

The cost of absorbing unskilled immigrants in a postmanufacturing America stings twice: once, because they compete for employment with low-skilled Americans already facing an economic crisis; and twice, because if they don't find employment while here, the social and economic cost to Americans is onerous. This is why I'm fiercely opposed to open borders and uncontrolled immigration. The elitist open-borders orthodoxy of the past few decades has hurt working Americans by allowing Big Business to import unlimited amounts of cheap labor. That's neither "tolerance" nor commitment to "diversity." It's a subsidy to corporate elites at the expense of working people and their families, and it has to stop.

Some elitists might concede all that and say: well yes, there is a problem with low-wage, unskilled immigration. That's why we should do more to enforce our borders and do more to require employers to verify the immigration status of their workers. We must clamp down on illegal immigration. But let's not shoot ourselves in the foot by restricting legal immigration: that's the part of the system where we really control the number and nature of the people who come here, and they contribute positively to our economy.

First of all: yes, of course we should enforce our borders and demand that Big Business isn't exploiting illegal immigrants for cheap labor. But the idea that the legal immigration system is working well is a far-fetched fantasy. Only one in fifteen legal immigrants comes to America for a job. Most legal immigration is family based. Again, of course I understand that. When we moved to America in support of my wife's career, we came as a family: my wife and me and our two children. But that was it. It didn't enter our heads that we would bring other family members with us. When my parents moved to the United Kingdom from Hungary, they didn't bring aunts, uncles, parents, and grandparents with them. That's not the deal. I don't know where this expectation comes from that wider family members should be part of the immigration package and then bring further extended family members in their own right.

But even the ostensibly most opportunity-focused part of the legal immigration system is full of abuse. One of the controlled immigration programs in place today is the H1-B visa, which was created to welcome immigrants with rare skills American employers couldn't source locally. In 2015, the *New York Times* reported that Disney laid off 250 employees and replaced them with Indians brought to the United States by an outsourcing firm on the H1-B visa program. Some of the laid-off Disney employees had to train their Indian replacements ... so how specialized were these Indians' skills, really? Their real value to Disney, it would seem, was their inability to create upward wage pressures the way American workers could. Most of the biggest users of the H1-B visa system are mass-outsourcing companies of the type used by Disney. It's a real, but typical, scandal: under the guise of bringing into America highly skilled workers who will contribute positively to the economy and help build economic opportunity for others, corporate America is hiring subcontractors to replace American workers with cheaper imported labor that can't pressure for wage increases, promotions, or leave to start their own business, under the condition of their visa.

Remember: none of this is the immigrants' fault, and we shouldn't blame or demonize them. I completely sympathize with Indians, Mexicans, Syrians, Hungarians, and any other immigrants in search of a better life for themselves in countries with stronger economies. They are pursuing opportunity for themselves and their families. But the positive populist believes that if charity begins at home, then so does opportunity, and our immigration system should be part of that; it should be designed to protect working Americans who are doing their best to support their own families and give them opportunity.

There are those who argue the open-borders case on a more macroeconomic level. They claim that gross domestic product (GDP) would soar if Americans disregarded their borders and let the forces of economic dynamism flow freely. But even if that's true (and it's worth remembering that labor is just one factor of production—infrastructure and innovation have a big impact, too), just because a nation's GDP is rising doesn't mean working- and middle-class people are benefiting. Big Business focuses on its bottom line, and idealistic libertarians focus on freedom of movement—but who is focusing on the people thrown on the scrap heap as skilled and unskilled immigrants take millions of available jobs in America?

Our country, like every other sovereign nation, is not just guaranteed the right to protect its territory; it's obligated to. A country without borders is no country at all. However, the positive populist rejects the harder edges of today's anti-immigrant rhetoric, which, if put into practice, could crush opportunity for working people by choking off one of our prime sources of innovation.

So the right policy solution is to combine the most rigorous elements of a controlled immigration system: an aggressive clampdown on illegal immigration and corporate illegal immigrant hiring by Big Business, a clampdown on visa programs and other forms of entry that are routinely abused—and combine this with a proactive hunt for the world's top talent to come to America and make their contribution to our economy and society. We should be rolling out the red carpet for students, entrepreneurs, scientists, artists—but only the best in the world—to come to the United States and renew America's unique story. That is the way to make sure immigration produces opportunity for all, not just a privileged few.

IN A NUTSHELL . . .

The globalists running our elitist economy treat workers like replaceable cogs, chips to move around a casino table. The Populist Economy demands radical reform to equip working Americans with the skills they need to have the opportunity to succeed on their own terms.

1. Radical school reform: Our centralized top-down factory school system is a relic of the nineteenth century. We need to sweep it away, replacing it with Universal Free Market Education that brings the best of educational innovation to everyone, not just the rich. Total school choice, fairly funded by a national voucher system.

2. Universal Free Market Training: We're done with the job-for-life days of old; every worker must have access to training through life, where necessary funded by government but provided in innovative and accessible ways by the market. Our goal should be employment security, not job security.

3. Opportunity immigration: Immigrants helped make America the most dynamic economy in the world, but not all immigration is productive. We must regain control of our borders, stop importing cheap labor that hurts American workers, and move to a market-based immigration system.

3

FAIRNESS

IF THERE'S ONE EMOTION that drives my kind of populism, it's a hatred of arbitrary and abusive power. I spent my childhood summers at my grandmother's home in Hungary, where in the twentieth century a communist government followed a fascist regime. My grandmother had been a respected and proud school-teacher until my mother fled to the West in the 1960s. In retaliation for her "bad parenting," the communist authorities stripped my grandmother of her beloved position, forcing her against a wall and publicly humiliating her in front of her colleagues and pupils. The government then imposed the cruelest punishment on her: she was banned from the teaching profession for life, and reassigned to a dark corner of a local museum as a guard. Nonetheless, she remained supportive of my mother's choice to leave Hungary in search of opportunity. Perhaps I get my deep-seated antipathy toward authoritarianism—or any kind of unfair or arbitrary authority—from my very tough grandmother.

It hasn't always been a helpful trait. Once when our high

school French teacher was more than half an hour late for class without explanation, I penned a letter of protest to him and led a class walkout. I was summoned to see the school's headmaster, who much to my surprise was more amused than angry, conceded that I had a point, but picked me up on my lack of etiquette. Somewhat improbably, he likened me to the then notorious union leader Arthur Scargill—at that time in the mid-1980s leading a fight-to-the-death miners' strike against the Thatcher government. (Ironically, a few years later I would in fact be working for Scargill's archnemesis, Mrs. Thatcher.)

Decades later, in another slightly ridiculous confrontation with authority, I managed to get myself arrested minutes after the end of the British Conservative Party's annual convention in the United Kingdom's second city, Birmingham. With the cheers of the audience still ringing in my ears for David Cameron's speech (mainly written by me), I got into an argument that, rather astonishingly, would end up leading the British TV news bulletins one day.

Desperate to catch a particular train that would get me back to London before my sons' bedtime, I rushed past the ticket inspectors airily waving my bag and shouting "the ticket's in here" (which indeed it was—all of us in the party leader's team had our travel arrangements made for us by our brilliant support staff). The inspectors didn't believe me (or, I like to think, were just being difficult because they could—there is no actual requirement to have your ticket checked before boarding as they are checked once you're on the train) and stopped me mid-rush. I started remonstrating and in the midst of all this a couple of burly British Transport Police officers came over to see what all the commotion was about. After a minute or so of high-octane argument one of the officers harshly grabbed my arm, to which I replied, "Get your hands off me, you wanker. . . ."

Next minute: I'm in handcuffs, being frog-marched across the station concourse with the officers accusing me of being drunk (didn't they realize we'd only just finished the party convention speech—the drinking was just about to start!). Given the fact that Britain is the most heavily surveilled place on earth, with CCTV cameras covering practically every inch of the country, my mind was already picturing that evening's news bulletins, where instead of my boss's triumphant speech viewers would be treated to his top aide being dragged across Birmingham New Street station in handcuffs. Fortunately, thanks to a timely intervention with the cops by the ever-resourceful Andy Coulson, at that time David Cameron's press secretary, I was "de-arrested" (whatever that means) and released. I missed my train—and an appearance on the news that night—but inevitably the media did eventually find out about the incident and enjoyed retelling the tale of the prime minister's right-hand man being arrested. It was satisfying, as you can imagine, to see the following headline in the *Daily Mail* a few years later: "End the bully tactics, train ticket inspectors are told in crackdown on passengers who are being 'treated like criminals.' . . ."

It's a silly story, and of course it pales into total insignificance when compared to the injustice, violence, and worse that many Americans without my privileges (and, let's be clear, skin color) experience at the hands of the police on a daily basis. But there's something deeper and more important that it signifies, and it relates not just to everyday interactions like that one with the police officers, not just to the way our society works, but to our economy as well—and it's an important driving force behind the populist rebellion.

Most people absolutely loathe the unfair exercise of power, and the disturbing truth is that the unfair exercise of power has become the hallmark of our elitist economy. You see it today in the way that corporations behave: the way they treat their employees, their customers, and their suppliers; and the way that our economic systems have become captured by the elite to entrench their advantages and keep upstart challengers out, whether that's new firms trying to crack open a market or a working-class person trying to climb the ladder.

Fairness is one of the foundational principles of the Populist Economy. We do not have a fair economy today: economic power is concentrated in too few hands, and when power is concentrated it is nearly always abused. That has to change, and the fight to change it is at the heart of Positive Populism.

American mythology places a great deal of emphasis on fairness and "equal protection under law"—certainly compared to many other nations. This might explain why, unlike some other cultures, for many years Americans trusted that whatever economic inequality exists is largely a fair outcome, the result of everyone playing by the same rules, with those who put the effort in getting their just rewards. In the past, American literature has celebrated the legions of poor people living virtuous lives and eventually working their way into the middle class, often rewarded with opportunities by the benevolent wealthy in their midst. Americans love success stories and rugged individualism. Millionaires—and billionaires—who are seen as having made it on their own are admired, and rightly so. What Americans don't love are those who get ahead by rigging the system, by circumventing the ground rules meant to guarantee basic fairness and equality of opportunity. And there is far too much of that going on these days.

It's not just offensive to people's sensibilities. It is economically counterproductive, too. A 2015 study by Columbia professor Jan Svejnar and Villanova professor Sutirtha Bagchi found that when billionaires' wealth was a result of entrepreneurism, their nation's economic growth wasn't harmed. This is proof that fair capitalism might lead to unequal outcomes, but isn't injurious. But when wealth is the result of political connections—such as when Russia and Mexico privatize state-owned assets and sell them to insiders at rock-bottom prices—their nation's economic growth does suffer because that is unfair capitalism, or cronyism.

Cronyism in the United States might not be as blatant as it is in Russia and Mexico, but Svejnar and Bagchi found that a greater percentage of US billionaires' wealth comes from political connections than does that of billionaires in Hong Kong, the Netherlands, Sweden, Switzerland, Singapore, and the United Kingdom. America is just not as fair as it should be—and could be. Just one proof point among many: AIG paid their retiring CEO Martin Sullivan $47 million in 2008, the same year American taxpayers paid $182 billion to bail the company out. Protestors targeted the homes of AIG executives near their Connecticut headquarters. JPMorgan and Citigroup bore similar scrutiny for their executive bonuses coupled with taxpayer bailouts. Occupy Wall Street rightly protested the unfairness; the 2014 publication of Thomas Picketty's *Capitalism in the 21st Century* provided more momentum. By October that year, Hillary Clinton was pandering to potential Bernie Sanders primary voters: "Don't let anyone tell you that, you know, it's corporations and business that create jobs," she pronounced at a campaign rally in Massachusetts.

What a classic example of her boneheadedness as a candidate: of course business creates jobs—the question is whether business does so in a way that commands popular support; in a way that's fair. For too long the debate around capitalism has been framed in a superficial way: you are "pro-business," in which case you're expected to be in favor of cutting taxes and regulations on the private sector and restricting the role and power of those who want to rein in the way corporations operate, like labor unions or certain pressure groups. Or you are "anti-business," in which case your sympathies are more with the public sector and you want to raise corporate taxes and control business behavior and decision making through government regulation.

This is such a dumb dichotomy. We should all be able to agree that business is a good thing, because it literally generates all the wealth that pays for individual and collective progress—not to mention generating the innovations that have transformed people's lives for the better all over the world: from medicines that cure disease to labor-saving devices that free people from domestic drudgery to the industries that put books like this in your hands.

Of course we should all be pro-business. When it comes to ensuring fair business, the real question is whether we are pro-market or not. It's market competition that provides one of the strongest checks on unfair business practices. Competition is not a silver bullet—even in strongly competitive markets, you can find unfairness that requires remedy. But we can surely state that uncompetitive markets where dominant players or monopolies can behave as they please without the threat of a competitor coming in to take their business away are the places where the worst excesses of capitalism are allowed to persist. This important distinction—between being pro-market and pro-business—is often lost, especially among conservatives and Republicans, many of whom have ended up being complacent about the way capitalism works in practice in twenty-first-century America.

The progressive left is actually more tuned into the nature of the problem. Bernie Sanders is absolutely correct when he talks about crony capitalism and a rigged system. But when this tips into anticapitalist sentiment, we part company. Billions of people have escaped poverty and have better lives because of the profits generated by capitalism. If businesses don't make a profit, they don't attract investors, and everybody loses. Without capitalism, government could not provide social safety nets, pensions, free education, healthcare. If we undermine the climate for business, we'll have less innovation, fewer jobs, fewer goods and services, and less money to help solve social problems. We need a practical, positive, constructive response to legitimate critiques of the way capitalism has gone haywire.

The positive populist aims to turn the rage against the "rigged system" (which is entirely justified) into reform, rather than punishment for "the rich." Our focus should be the rules—and the interpretation of those rules by the courts and the bureaucracy—that have allowed an unacceptable concentration of power in our economy, with corporations getting bigger and bigger and thereby being in a stronger and stronger position to stifle challengers and behave abusively. This concentration of power has made it harder for upstarts with good ideas and determination to enter new markets and challenge incumbents. It has allowed Big Business to get away with increasingly unfair labor practices that crush the opportunities of working Americans. And it has left industry after industry dominated by a handful of big players who act in ways that hurt the public interest. All this must be swept away in the Populist Economy of the future.

The right kind of regulation for capitalism doesn't necessarily mean more rules—it can also mean fewer, better rules that regulate the structure of the market and not the behavior of individual players within that market. Competition is what makes free markets fair. It's the concentration of power that enables our system to be rigged. If we attack that concentration of power, we can readjust the playing field so it tilts instead toward working Americans—on taxes, on regulations, on every aspect of our economy. We need to start by completely rethinking our attitude to antitrust.

1. BRING BACK BRANDEISIANISM

President Theodore Roosevelt and Senator John Sherman saw the abuses of America's early industrialists and understood the importance of robust market competition. They took on the monopolists of the Gilded Age, breaking up the railroads, Big Steel, and Big Oil so that every American could have a "square deal": "When I say that I am for the square deal, I mean not merely that I stand for fair play under the present rules of the game, but that I stand for having those rules changed so as to work for a more substantial equality of opportunity and of reward for equally good service," President Roosevelt explained in his 1910 New Nationalism address to residents of Osawatomie, Kansas.

Although Roosevelt is the American leader most associated in popular imagination with the antitrust movement, perhaps the single figure in our national story who did most to turn pro-market, antimonopolistic impulses into an intellectually coherent and operationally tangible agenda was Supreme Court justice Louis Brandeis. Before his appointment to the Court in 1916, he had become known as "the people's lawyer" for his work to attack corporate abuses of consumers and workers, including a six-year battle to prevent J. P. Morgan from monopolizing New England railroads. His philosophy was summed up in one of his dissenting opinions where he condemned "the gross inequality in the distribution of wealth and income which giant corporations have festered." He argued for restrictions on the "concentration of wealth and power" in the name of democracy, just as much as consumer welfare.

But Teddy Roosevelt's trust-busting crusade and Louis Brandeis's bracing pursuit of it didn't last. Over the course of the twentieth century, businesses got bigger and bigger, economic power more and more concentrated. This trend was accelerated by World War II and its associated sense of urgent, large-scale national effort. But the real transformation happened in the 1970s, led by the "modern" theories of left-wing economists like J. K. Galbraith who argued that giant corporations run through management science were in the public interest, and even more so by the conservative Robert Bork, who argued, based on the theories of the Chicago school of economics, that the only factor in evaluating antitrust cases should be consumer welfare. This thinking has influenced legal scholars from the lower rungs of the bar all the way up to the Supreme Court, which has increasingly turned a blind eye to the consolidation of economic power. Bard professor Walter Russell Mead brilliantly captures the complacency that resulted from this neglect:

> The "commanding heights" of American business were controlled by a small number of sometimes monopolistic, usually oligopolistic firms. AT&T, for example, was the only serious telephone company in the country, and both the services it offered and the prices it charged were tightly regulated by the government. The Big Three automakers had a lock on the car market. . . . there was virtually no foreign competition.
>
> A handful of airlines divided up the routes and the market; airlines could not compete by offering lower prices or by opening new routes without government permission. Banks, utilities, insurance companies and trucking companies had their rates and, essentially, their profit levels set by Federal regulators.
>
> This stable economic structure allowed a consistent division of the pie. Unionized workers, then a far larger per-

centage of laborers than is the case today, got steady raises in steady jobs. The government got a steady flow of tax revenues. Shareholders got reasonably steady dividends.

More recently, the rise of America's technology sector has unleashed a new specter of monopoly, driven by the logic of the venture capital industry. As I now know from personal experience, investors in technology companies, when they hear pitches from eager entrepreneurs, are not actually evaluating whether or not the proposed business is likely to be successful. They know that at least 90 percent of the businesses they back will fail. Investors' principal question is: "If this business succeeds, will it command a big enough share of a big enough market to deliver monopolistic returns on a massive scale?" They call it "network effects"—the more people who use a tech product, the more valuable it becomes to existing and new users, with a very clear goal in mind: make literally everyone a user, squeezing out every competitor. The explicit pursuit of monopoly is in Silicon Valley's DNA.

This private reality is in sharp contrast to the public narrative. For two decades we've been told that the tech sector is essentially a digital manifestation of the David-and-Goliath story. We needn't worry about companies growing too big and powerful, because the costs of starting and scaling a tech business are falling all the time. Small start-ups can disrupt giants practically overnight. Look at how Microsoft toppled IBM; then Google toppled Microsoft. Facebook toppled Myspace. But then look at how Facebook, fearing disruption first by Instagram and then WhatsApp, crushed the competition not by beating it but buying it. Amazon's disruption of booksellers, shopping malls, and now even national grocery chains is well-known. Less well-known is its takeover of vast swaths of the Internet's infrastructure with its cloud-computing service

AWS. Yes, there is sharp competition for cloud computing. But where is it coming from? Google and Microsoft, the other tech giants. The fact is that anyone wanting to start a tech company now is dependent on these solidly entrenched behemoths: Facebook advertising to reach your customers, Google search to be found by them, Apple for your app, Amazon for your data. And if a new start-up is successful, the ambition of tech founders these days has shifted from the romantic dream of toppling the incumbents to the more prosaic but highly lucrative one of being acquired by them.

None of this is to deny the genius of the founders and leaders of the technology giants (full disclosure: at the time of my writing my wife is a senior executive at Facebook and was previously at Uber and Google). But as they balloon in size and weight, competition and resulting economic growth is slowing down. "It's not a coincidence that at a time when the startup rate is in a long-term decline, the economy has not grown at 3 percent or better," John Dearie of the Center for American Entrepreneurship told the *Guardian*. "The reason why this is so troubling is that new businesses account for virtually all new job creation and account disproportionately for disruptive innovations."

The technology sector is just one example of a market with too little competition. Alongside Big Tech we have the Big Banks, Big Pharma, Big Food, Big Agriculture . . . the insurance companies, the airlines, the beer and spirits industry . . . in many communities you see it even in fast food. One of my economics tutors at Oxford told me pithily that it's the aim of every business to become a monopoly. Maybe—but it should be our aim to stop them.

Until now, our approach to that challenge has been tactical, piecemeal, and arbitrary. Individual mergers and acquisitions may or may not be challenged by government authorities depending on the prevailing political wisdom—or whim—of the moment. Individual judges may rule for or against them, with no guiding principle to fall back on—judicial approaches have lurched wildly over the years. And individual sectors may from time to time be singled out for attention: "Let's break up the banks!" Yes, let's—but why not the health insurance companies, too, since that's an even more concentrated market?

Of course you will often find the entrenched incumbents in a particular sector protected by the politicians they sustain with political donations and, later, lucrative board seats and consultancies. The board seats and consultancies are handed out to the bureaucrats, too, and the whole gang of elitist insiders conspire to spin a tale about how important it is to have big corporations in this or that industry on "national security" grounds, or because it's good to have national champions that can stand up to foreign competition. It's all self-serving nonsense.

In addition, a damaging ideology has taken hold that serves the elite but hurts everyone else: the prioritization of consumer welfare. Robert Bork's argument has become accepted as axiomatic: concentrations of economic power are perfectly fine as long as consumers are not harmed. If prices are low and consumers are being well served then all is fine and dandy. Big is not bad: it's efficient. This is an extraordinarily narrow, shortsighted, and, frankly, grim view of the world. We are not just consumers, we are citizens, too. We are employees. We are neighbors. We are humans, and humans are not defined by "efficiency."

We need to bring some order, predictability, and above all humanity to antitrust, based on a positive populist bias against the unfairness and social harm that comes from excessive market power, regardless of its efficiency in delivering consumer welfare. A revolutionary way to do that is to make the antitrust system more like the tax system, with different policy treatment for different rates of market concentration. By harnessing the most important public policy drivers for businesses, regulation and taxation, we can create powerful incentives for greater competition and less concentration.

For example, we could set three bands: above 50 percent market share makes you a utility—basically part of the public sector. You will face onerous and highly interventionist regulation on every aspect of your business: maximum pay rates for senior executives, minimum pay rates for employees, a maximum ratio for top to median pay, requirements on community investment, the highest rate of corporate tax. Between 10 percent and 50 percent you are defined as a dominant player—with many of the same kinds of requirements imposed as on utilities but with a less onerous regulatory burden and a lower rate of tax. Below 10 percent you are deemed to be competitive: free of most regulation and with no corporate tax burden at all. Such a system would create powerful incentives against monopolistic ambitions.

Of course, all the elements in such a framework could and would be contested: Why three bands? Why at those levels? How do you define a market—Amazon would be in one category if described as a "retailer," another if seen as an "online retailer," and another again if defined as a "book retailer." Fine—let's argue about all that. But at least we will have a framework for the argument, and at least it will be based on simple, comprehensible ideas: that we believe in fairness, that fair capitalism is competitive capitalism, and that the days of turning a blind eye to elitist power grabs are over.

2. NO MORE NONCOMPETES

Whether or not we manage to put in place a comprehensive antitrust regime such as the one outlined above, there are specific instances of corporate unfairness that we should attend to in their own right. One of these is the scandal of noncompete agreements, explicitly designed by crony businesses to exploit their workers and rob them of their agency, dignity, and right to a fair wage. During the Great Recession, unemployment in the United States reached 10 percent, but ten years later it had fallen to around 4 percent, the level that economists in their esoteric way like to describe as "full employment." Why, then, haven't wages risen along with employment? Whatever happened to the laws of supply and demand? Break it gently to the useless economists slaving over their "models" in their ivory towers: there's a thing called the real world. And in it, when it comes to the workplace, corporations rig the laws of supply and demand in their favor.

Almost one-fifth of American workers labor under "noncompete" agreements, which were once the domain of highly compensated employees privy to trade secrets or in possession of a golden Rolodex. But now blue-collar and entry-level employees are told that if they leave to work for a competitor, it will result in legal action against them . . . even if they are bringing nothing to the next employer except their own acquired skills. According to *Time*, 14 percent of people earning less than $40,000 are subjected to these agreements. And 70 percent of the time, the agreements were presented to them only after they had accepted the job.

It's long been the case that the fastest way to negotiate a raise from an employer is to prove what you're worth on the open market by procuring another offer of employment. But in making low-wage earners sign noncompete agreements, employers are robbing them of that essential leverage. Most people can't afford to hire an attorney to review the noncompete clauses, never mind fight to get them out of their contracts. Franchise agreements can be another unfair employer practice used to limit the mobility and leverage of entry-level workers. Companies such as Burger King, Pizza Hut, Jiffy Lube, and Curves have management-level agreements that employees don't even see or sign—but that prevent them from hiring employees who worked at other locations.

We like to think of entry-level jobs as a stepping-stone to bigger and better things. But if workers can't benefit from the open market's supply-and-demand effect on wages, how are they to advance? Perhaps their skills are valued more highly at a different location of the same chain; shouldn't we be encouraging this kind of growth instead of blocking it? With fewer options available to them on the job market, wage earners are trapped—in these cases, they can't just leave for a competitor willing to pay them more. This situation has the effect of changing the employer/employee relationship into a master/servant one, where employers get away with dictating employees' personal behavior.

In *More Human* I wrote about the tendency of big companies to centralize power for the sake of efficiency and quantifiable results, but at significant cost to employees, who are stripped of their discretion and autonomy. Compound this tendency with the advantage employers have over employees, knowing they can't just quit and find another job, and you have incidents of employers abusing employees by depriving them of bathroom breaks, searching their personal belongings, and penalizing them for smoking off the premises, speaking their mind politically, and who knows what else.

There are many other examples of workplace unfairness, including the imposition of mandatory arbitration for employment claims, arbitrary and unpredictable scheduling, and the way in which corporations can absolve themselves of responsibility for employment conditions through subcontracting. All these assaults on working people by the elite are made easier by the decline of union membership in the private sector. Growing up in the union-ravaged economy of 1970s Great Britain, I absorbed a cultural hostility to organized labor. And that's still partly with me in America today as I observe, for example, the way in which public-sector unions destroy life chances for poor and working-class families in my home state of California by siphoning off resources and blocking reform. But in the private sector, it's hard to argue against the need for more worker protection. More unionization, or at least a modern form of it, could be part of the answer.

University of Michigan professor Elizabeth Anderson, who has meticulously documented employers' abusive and unfair labor practices, concedes that Americans shy away from private-sector labor unions because they "prefer a collaborative to an adversarial relationship" with their employers. But a "codetermination" system like the one in Germany, whereby employees elect representatives to the board of directors and serve on a council governing workplace issues, can be a positive populist model for good business. We need to outlaw noncompete agreements, as California has, along with the other instances of unfairness that plague American workers today, and mandate workplace democracy throughout the economy—while leaving each company to decide the most suitable form it should take.

3. BREAKING DOWN BARRIERS

There's one more specific type of elitist unfairness that we need to tackle, and that's the way in which insiders protect their interests and keep everyone else out by building barriers. It happens with industries and individual companies, and it even happens at the personal level, too, as we shall see. The Populist Economy is one in which the bias is in favor of the upstart, the challenger, the outsider. That's a long way from where we are today.

If you wanted to start a new company that would lower costs and offer superior service in a struggling industry, and you already had a proven track record of success in another country, you'd think such an enterprise would be welcomed in the United States. That's not the experience the subsequently top-rated airline Virgin America had when it tried to enter the American market in 2005. The existing airlines with a monopoly on domestic routes lobbied Washington against Virgin and blocked its application to the Department of Transportation.

Just four years earlier, these very airlines had gone hat in hand to Congress asking for money, blaming the events of September 11, 2001, for their poor financial condition. Taxpayers bailed out the airlines with a package totaling $15 billion. Nonetheless, the airlines continued to crumble, going bankrupt, merging, raising fares, canceling routes, and defaulting on their employees' pensions. And yet an airline willing to base itself in California and employ 3,000 people, and offering to "put the fun back in flying" with lower fares, stylish new planes, and customer-pleasing staff, was rejected. What Virgin America had to do, according to the Wharton Business School's journal *Knowledge,* is outrageous:

> To help win regulatory approval, [Virgin America] hired lobbyists and enlisted support from numerous politicians, including then-senator Hillary Clinton, California senator Diane Feinstein, Arnold Schwarzenegger (former governor of California) and Gavin Newsom (former mayor of San Francisco).

Is it any wonder that 50 percent of senators become lobbyists after they leave government, and 42 percent of congressmen do— up from just 3 percent in 1974? As government barriers to entry have grown more forbidding and complex, so has the demand for insiders who know how to navigate them, at every level of government. By the end of 2007, Washington regulators changed course and allowed Virgin America into the market. A decade later, it was swallowed up by a rival, Alaska Airlines.

THE BIG CAR COMPANIES like General Motors and Chrysler are just as bad as the big airlines. In 2009, they begged Congress for a bailout and were loaned almost $80 billion—$9 billion of which they failed to repay. (At least they are still in business, their supporters argued.) But part of the way they do business is by trying to block newcomers like Tesla from entering the automotive industry. The overwhelming majority of states have laws banning the direct sale of cars from manufacturers to customers, giving big car dealerships a lot of political power. But Teslas are not like other car dealers—the vehicles are all-electric, run by constantly evolving software, and Tesla needs quick customer feedback that can only come from having a direct relationship with its customers. Tesla has a long list of consumers waiting to buy their vehicles as soon as they are produced, and by early 2017 it had become the most valuable car company in America, surpassing both Ford and GM.

The major automotive companies, who couldn't even stay in business without taxpayer subsidies, joined with car dealerships to lobby (and bribe) state legislatures to block Tesla's disruptive model. Who is hurt by this? Regular people who work for Tesla. People who want to buy Tesla's cars (which start at $35,000) but are forbidden from purchasing or servicing a Tesla in their own state. If the barriers to entry are this high for companies like Virgin and Tesla, run by charismatic billionaires like Sir Richard Branson and Elon Musk, how does a regular entrepreneur surmount them? Every day you read another story about the costly licenses and mandatory courses demanded of people who want to start a business doing African-style hair braiding, or selling homemade food from a truck, or giving tours of city neighborhoods. This isn't a competitive capitalist system—this is an arbitrary exercise of power by those who have connections in government. We need to change the bias in our system from protecting the incumbent to helping the challenger.

There's another pernicious aspect of this elitist insiderism, and it's personal. One of the ways that elitists entrench their privileges is by literally putting each other into positions of power and influence and keeping outsiders out. All that letter writing, lobbying, and bribing with donations to get kids a college place. All those internships and board seats handed out to the protected and connected.

This kind of know-your-place mentality belongs in nineteenth-century England, not twenty-first-century America. Fairness in our economy means outlawing these discriminatory elitist practices. Colleges must be legally prevented from taking account of personal connections, lobbying, or donations when it comes to admissions. Internships and board positions should be awarded on the basis of open competition: what you can do, not who you know.

I know from personal experience that the elite will fight like hell against these changes. One of the most vicious arguments I witnessed during my time in government was about this very issue. Our administration had made multiple public commitments to the goal of advancing social mobility. Nick Clegg, deputy prime minister and leader of our coalition partner the Liberal Democrats, was formally responsible for overseeing the government's social mobility strategy. One of his more modest, but absolutely correct, proposals was for the government itself to practice what it preached: he wanted to ban government ministers and civil servants from offering internships in an informal, closed manner— you know the kind of thing, where the positions are handed out to children of friends, godchildren and the like, so no one without the right connections gets a look-in. All of us in the policy staff thought this was a good, sensible, and fundamentally uncontroversial proposal. But then it reached the prime minister's desk. David Cameron reacted with total fury and vowed to block it at any cost. It was at that moment that I saw the ferocity with which the elite guards its way of life.

They must be defeated. The Populist Economy is a fair economy, where everyone has a chance to compete: every entrepreneur, every ambitious young person chasing opportunity. We must tear down the barriers that the elite have put in place to protect their privileged position.

IN A NUTSHELL . . .

Competition is what makes free markets fair. But elitism has grown and fortified the advantages of the insiders and the establishment, in business and other walks of life. We should break up the power of Big Business and break down the barriers in the way of small business. We must move aggressively to build a Populist Economy that's fair for entrepreneurs and workers.

1. Bring back Brandeisianism: Teddy Roosevelt and Louis Brandeis's trust-busting agenda helped end the Gilded Age and set the stage for a century of American prosperity; we need a new and forceful antitrust regime that follows in their footsteps to end the Elitist Age in today's economy. The less competition corporations face, the greater the constraints that should be placed on their behavior and the more they should pay in tax. Big corporations in uncompetitive markets should be treated like public utilities; if they want the privileges of free and fair market competition, they should break themselves up.

2. No more noncompetes: Employers have always held power over their workers, but by using noncompete agreements to block employees from working in the same industry for essentially made-up reasons, they keep wages down and job mobility low. It's time to outlaw noncompetes and bring democracy to the workplace.

3. Breaking down barriers: Incumbent big businesses will stop at nothing to prevent insurgent start-ups and competitors. We need to change the system to favor those who are fighting to get to the top, not those who are already there.

THE
POPULIST
SOCIETY

TOO MANY POPULISTS FOCUS ONLY ON QUESTIONS OF economics. Of course, those questions are vital, but it's not the whole story, not by a long way. There's more to life than money and even if we solve the massive problems of economic insecurity, declining opportunity, and rampant unfairness, the work of Positive Populism will not be done.

Why? Because populism is about people, and people are not just economic units, they are social animals. And the truth is, our society is broken, our social fabric frayed.

This is about much more than the oft-debated phenomena of political and cultural polarization. Yes, it's true that America is divided. But divergent attitudes and ideologies are superficial problems compared to the things that really matter: the building blocks of a strong society—family, community, country. The top 20 percent of American families and communities might prosper on their own, but for the rest, the traditional structures of support have fallen by the wayside. Families are crumbling, under assault from blistering economic forces, technological experiments, and social changes that are the enemy of stable relationships. Communities, once redoubts of solidarity and civic pride, have become atomized, making us too often strangers in our own neighborhoods. And rather than unite us in the dignity of a shared national story, the long-unbreakable ties of flag and country are now more likely to cause discord than inspire us.

This is not inevitable. Family, community, and the positive inspiration of country are all alive and well in pockets of America, and there are decisive actions we can take to rebuild them everywhere. For positive populists, "family values" aren't about sex and prudishness but giving families the tools to stay together and succeed. It *does* take a village to raise a child, and we mustn't push family out of the public sphere. Technology has helped intensify division and isolation but it has also given us new ways to create connections; let's use it to catalyze local engagement, too. And even if the elites have cut loose from the ties of country, it doesn't minimize the importance of the nation-state. We succeed as a nation; citizenship and sovereignty matter, even in today's globalized world. Perhaps even more.

We should aspire to a society that's more human, that works together to solve problems, where we support one another. The Populist Society doesn't just fill the gaps left by government—it takes the initiative.

4

FAMILY

I REMEMBER THE MOMENT with total clarity. I had just kissed my eldest son good night, leaving the door slightly ajar as usual. I walked toward the top of the stairs, about to head back downstairs, as usual. And then it suddenly hit me: he's four. He's exactly the age I was when my father left us. *How could he have done that?*

I didn't (and don't) ask that question in a hostile or even judgmental way, but in a genuine spirit of inquiry. I didn't really know my father—I have just a few memories from the vacations we took together when I would visit him in Hungary for a couple of weeks at a time. But even so, there must have been some kind of connection, because when his regular letters to me suddenly stopped when I was around eleven or twelve, I remember going on a rather sad and ultimately fruitless hunt for him the next time I visited my mother's side of the family. They live in a small town in southern Hungary, Szeged, and on this particular trip I insisted on taking the train up to Budapest on my own to try to find my father. I just couldn't understand why he would have stopped writing. I remember going to the last address I had for him, but there was no one there and nobody had seen him for a while. I asked around to see if there was a new address I could try, but no one I spoke to had any idea. Eventually I gave up and made the trip back down to Szeged. A few years later, I found out that he had been dead for a number of years—including on that day I went looking for him.

I still don't know all the circumstances but apparently he got ill, didn't have anyone to look after him, and didn't want me to see him in the condition he was in. When he died, the only next of kin the authorities in Hungary had was my half sister, by then in her fifties, who lived in Australia. She flew out to deal with the arrangements and in the rush of trying to sort everything out forgot to tell me or my mother what had happened. After a week or so, she felt so embarrassed that she thought she couldn't just make a quick phone call; she'd need to come and see us to explain. But that wasn't possible for her . . . the weeks turned into months, and then years. Eventually we met and she told me to my face that my father had died a few years before.

I can't possibly know, and never will, what my father felt when he left. I'm just saying that when I reached the equivalent point in my own family, the idea of walking out on a four-year-old child was unimaginable. That must surely be true for most fathers. And yet, despite the incredible pain of leaving a child, it has become increasingly common over the past few decades for parents, mostly fathers, to do just that.

Perhaps because of that childhood experience, the issue of family became central to my political identity. In fact, one of the strongest bonds in my political and personal connection with David Cameron was the importance of family. "Family," he said at the first party convention that he addressed as Conservative leader, "is the most important thing in my life, and it should be the most important thing in our nation's life too." I wrote it; he said it; we both meant it.

For many years before, discussion of family policy in British politics had been somewhat taboo. It had become tainted by the phrase "family values," associated with a certain kind of censoriousness, priggishness, smugness. Not to mention a good dose of hypocrisy, too, as the very politicians who most enjoyed lecturing everyone else on family values often turned out—as we discovered thanks to the determined exertions of the British tabloid press—to have personal family arrangements of the more exotic variety. There was an establishment consensus that politicians should steer clear of "the family," that it represented a level of moral preaching best left to the church.

The trouble was, the church wasn't doing it. You were more likely to hear the Church of England express a strong opinion on climate change or poverty in Africa than the state of family life in Britain. That's despite the growing weight of evidence from longitudinal data, social policy research, and more recently from breakthroughs in neuroscience, that family background is the single most important factor in determining a child's life chances. From both personal and professional perspectives, Cameron and I saw just how vital an issue the family was. And yet no one was really talking about it. We felt a burning need to fill the gap: to speak out, to speak plainly, and to make family policy a top priority.

I feel that same burning need to speak out in America today. In fact it's even stronger, because the situation is even worse. More and more children in America are growing up in broken homes and in a culture of toxic stress and violence. Most of these children will never commit a crime. But many will end up living in poverty. Suffering addiction. Or homelessness, or debt, or persistent unemployment—or a combination of these things—trapping them in lives without any of the opportunities that others take for granted. The causal connection between family breakdown and the intractable social issues that form the core of our political debates—taxes and government spending, inequality, crime—is well researched and well established. The science is in. It's just that we don't want to confront it because it means confronting something that is very personal to each of us: how we choose to live our lives.

The elephant in the room is marriage. The data shows clearly that on average, children who are raised in stable homes with both parents do better. Children from divorced parents, or whose parents never married in the first place, do worse—whether that's in terms of lower levels of social mobility or higher levels of poverty. Of course, averages have exceptions to them. Many children from broken homes do well. I'm one of them.

But that doesn't make it the best way for children to be raised. And I don't understand why we as a society *wouldn't* want to do all we can to make sure children are raised in the best way possible. It strikes me as being intellectually lazy—even callous—to be agnostic on the question, especially given the scale of what has happened in recent decades.

Up until around sixty years ago, fewer than 10 percent of children were born to parents who weren't married. Today that proportion has more than quadrupled, to nearly half of all births. I myself contributed to the tally in the United Kingdom: Rachel and I were only married six months after the birth of our first son. But we did actually get married. And here's why all this matters, in its own right and in relation to populism: if your parents never married each other, you have roughly half the chance of moving up the ladder of economic progress.

It's even worse if your parents divorced, as my own did. Then you have a quarter of the chance of advancing from the bottom third of the income ladder. Things start to look better, however, if you're born to parents who are married. Then, if you're born into a family in the bottom third, there's a *50 percent* chance that you will grow up to occupy a place in the middle third or the top third of the ladder, according to a forty-year-long study released by Pew Research in 2010. But marriage, despite its clear benefits, is a rarity these days. In 1960, nearly three-quarters of children were living with both of their parents. By 2014 it was fewer than half, one of the biggest and most sudden social changes in all of human history. For a variety of reasons, parents no longer feel a sense of social pressure to get married before their children are born—and children are suffering as a result.

Numerous studies show children of divorced parents suffer divorces themselves at significantly higher rates than those whose parents remained married. Whatever their income level, children of divorced parents tend to suffer from a higher incidence of uncooperativeness in school, aggressive behavior, and depression throughout their lives. In America, the divorce rate has leveled off since its heyday in the 1980s, but that good news has been offset by fewer people bothering to marry in the first place before having children together. Instead, there has been a deterioration in social indicators of many kinds—from higher incarceration rates to substance abuse to educational attainment.

My populist passion may in part be the result of succeeding despite the odds stacked against me as the product of a divorced home led, for a while at least, by a single mother. And it was these experiences, contrasted with David Cameron's stable childhood home life, that led us to place an emphasis on family. We based a whole range of positive policy ideas on the simple premise that a stable, married family is the single most effective way to fight poverty, reduce inequality, and maximize opportunity.

That's why family policy is the single most important issue to get right. Strong families are the foundation of a strong, prosperous society. That makes family a populist issue. But it shouldn't be a partisan one. If your focus is individual freedom and reducing the size and scope of government, it's not enough to cut things back and hope for the best. Simply reducing the supply of government won't, pardon the pun, cut it. You also have to reduce the *demand* for government. You have to actually solve the social problems that give rise to so much of what government does and what it spends so much money on.

If your focus is social justice and reducing poverty and inequality, it is now evident that spending money on these problems is not enough. We've been doing that from the New Deal in the 1930s through to the Great Society in the 1960s and beyond. If anything the problems are worse, not better. The fight needs to be taken to the *underlying causes* of poverty and inequality, not just the symptoms.

Whichever way you look at it, you end up in the same place: the family. The single best thing we can do to extend opportunity, raise incomes, build a fairer society, fight crime and drug addiction, improve health, reduce welfare—you name it—is try to design policies that make sure every child in America is raised in a stable, loving home.

Sounds so simple, but this goal has proved unattainable. That's because traditional politics get in the way. At least since the start of the Culture Wars, the right has championed "family values" but shied away from any kind of proactive role for government in helping to strengthen families. Ideological opposition to a "nanny state" has often precluded consideration of practical programs, like paid parental leave or universal pre-K, that would end up helping to achieve fundamentally conservative ends: fewer out-of-wedlock births, less divorce, more community stability.

The left, meanwhile, has always championed women, children, and working families but shied away from anything that could be interpreted as a judgment on people's personal choices. Vice President Dan Quayle tried to scold the media elite for glamorizing single motherhood with the 1990s television program *Murphy Brown,* and he was mocked by elitists for promulgating those outmoded "family values." Establishment politicians took note of the backlash, and resolved, as their counterparts in the United Kingdom had done, not to express an opinion about others' lifestyle choices.

This abdication of responsibility from all our political leaders has been a disaster for America, seen in rising levels of family breakdown that have entrenched disadvantage and created a broken society.

And here we come back to the tricky territory that David Cameron and I tried to navigate. Many of our closest Conservative Party colleagues at the time told us to steer clear. Some even signaled to their fellow elitists in the media that they were privately uncomfortable "with all this family stuff." I lost count of the number of times I would sit around a fancy dinner table in one of the richest neighborhoods in London and be patronizingly informed by some snooty member of the cultural elite that she and her partner weren't married but look how well their (privately educated!) children had turned out. Or by another, that his highly civilized divorce and remarriage hadn't in any way jeopardized their delightful offspring's gilded path to Oxford University and a marvelous job in the media. Of course it's true that family breakdown has a different impact on families with different incomes. For example, a well-paid professional woman can more easily afford to raise children independently; but the rest struggle, as my own mother did. We should surely be more interested in progress for those at the bottom than pandering to those at the top.

So it's time to turn things around. A positive populist agenda for families would ignore ideological constraints and put in place the practical support that modern families need to thrive and flourish.

1. ACTIVELY SUPPORT MARRIAGE AND FAMILIES

There is much to celebrate in the various social, cultural, and political emancipations of the 1960s and '70s. Some of the slogans were burned into the consciousness of the time: "A woman needs a man like a fish needs a bicycle," "I'm as free as a bird now, and this bird you cannot change."

But there's a "but."

One of the most important voices to admit that those attitudes were not just liberating but in certain vital respects caused significant societal damage is Princeton professor Sara McLanahan, one of the principal investigators of the Fragile Families research project, run by Princeton and Columbia. In her 2004 academic paper "Diverging Destinies," she writes:

> Whereas children who were born to the most-educated women are gaining resources, in terms of parents' time and money, those who were born to the least-educated women are losing resources. . . . Although some analysts have argued that single motherhood is an indicator of women's greater economic independence and parity with men, the rejection of this status by college-educated women suggests otherwise. . . .

In other words, educated women marry more and divorce less, and that's good for their children. I wholeheartedly agree—and as the supportive husband of a woman with a spectacularly successful career who has for many years earned more than me, I assure you that I do not see this as an agenda to return to the 1950s. Quite the opposite.

One of the great ironies of the modern age is the fact that just as society has embraced—and made a legal reality of—marriage equality, the institution that progressives champion for gay people has seen a dramatic collapse when it comes to heterosexual couples, especially those at the lower end of the income scale. Barely a quarter of poor Americans aged eighteen to fifty-five are married, compared to more than half of their middle- and upper-class peers. Those divisions would be even more pronounced were it not for the working-class immigrant families who are disproportionately headed by married couples. These days, marriage is basically for rich people and for gay people. That's not good for our society: I want it to be for everybody. As I've often said, I strongly support marriage equality; in fact I support it so much I even think straight people should get married if they want to have children.

And that last part is crucial. Frankly, it is nobody's business but their own if couples with no intention of starting a family get married or not. It's entirely up to them. But the minute that children come into the picture, it's different, for the very simple and obvious reason that the way children are raised affects society as a whole, not just the individuals directly involved. We can't just privatize the issue of marriage. It's an issue of social responsibility, not just personal choice. For too long now, our culture has prioritized the personal choices of parents rather than the long-term interests of children and the impact of parental choices on society.

Why does marriage matter so much? Because the evidence points to a clear conclusion: children who grow up in homes with both married parents have better outcomes in life. As Professor McLanahan showed: "The vast majority of children born to unmarried parents experience a great deal of family instability and complexity, defined as families composed of half siblings and stepsiblings," she writes. "These families require a great deal of time and energy to manage, and the children in these families do less well than children in stable two-parent families, especially in terms of their social and emotional development."

Maybe, you might say. But can't unmarried parents offer stability? Can't a single parent offer stability? Yes, of course they can—but it's a question of what is *more likely* to produce the best conditions for a child to flourish. And the role of marriage in creating stability is impossible to ignore. Parents are much more likely to stay together as a couple if they are married. McLanahan finds: "While most of the unwed couples in the survey were living together or dating at the birth of their child, 61 percent of the couples had broken up by the child's fifth birthday. The families of unmarried parents experienced a great deal of instability in relationships, as mothers and fathers broke up, formed new relationships and, in many cases, had children with new partners." Other studies tell the same story: roughly two-thirds of children born to cohabiting parents will see them break up by the time they're twelve; for married parents it's around a quarter. That's a huge difference.

For the positive populist, marriage is not a moral matter: it is a deeply practical one. Your response to the data on breakups might be: isn't that because people who have stronger relationships are just more likely to get married, and less likely to break up? Actually, if you look at evidence from behavioral economics and social psychology, there is something deeper going on. Marriage is what behavioral psychologists call a commitment device; the very act of declaring and formalizing your bond makes it more likely you will stick together as a couple through all the inevitable stresses and tensions of raising a family. It's a commitment device, by the way, that not only improves the lives of children but of adults, too. Married people tend to live longer, have fewer strokes and heart attacks, have a lower chance of becoming depressed, are less likely to have advanced cancer when they're diagnosed, and are more likely to survive cancer or a major operation. They even have more sex. (Apparently.)

So if we accept that marriage is a good thing and worth encouraging, how exactly can we do that? For many years, social (and other) conservatives have advocated community and faith-based programs, such as Marriage Savers or Community Marriage Covenants—and there are many worthy efforts like these. But with the best will in the world, it is hard to describe their impact as anything other than modest. Of course we should continue to support and encourage such initiatives—but frankly, the scale of the problem deserves a serious public policy response.

What possible role can public policy play in something so deeply personal? Well—there absolutely are things we can do: practical things, not preaching. It's all about understanding the human reality of people's lives and the small steps that can lead to a big decision like breaking up your family (or deciding to start one without being married in the first place).

The first thing government can do to support marriage and families is to adopt the famous Hippocratic injunction to doctors: "First, do no harm." Those who hate the very idea of "the government" "interfering" in people's "private lives" might care to reflect on the fact that the government is already doing exactly that, and in a deeply unhelpful way. The government is not neutral when it comes to marriage. It actively discourages it, particularly through the welfare system, with almost one in three Americans reporting that they personally know someone who has not married because they were worried about losing means-tested benefits. It is completely absurd for government to design any of its services in a way that discourages marriage; it's like making an own-goal. Policy makers should heed the numerous proposals from think tanks and others for remedying these counterproductive policies. And when introducing new policies—for example, the Business-Friendly Living Wage described in Chapter 1—government should use them to incentivize, not penalize, marriage.

But there are other, more positive ways government can help couples who are planning to have children to come together and stay together. One example is through modernizing our attitude to work and family, to reflect the fact that most households need both parents to work in order to make ends meet, and that increasingly the main breadwinner in a traditional family is just as likely to be the woman as it is the man. For these reasons and more, we need to advance a family-friendly agenda throughout the world of work, and to back the idea of shared parenting. Married couples that share home responsibilities and breadwinning report higher levels of happiness and life satisfaction than other families, according to a 2009 University of Western Ontario study. During my time working in government in the United Kingdom, I pushed for more paternity leave for fathers so they could bond longer with their babies, forming stronger attachments that might help keep families together. Ensuring all parents can take sufficient leave should be at the heart of any family-friendly agenda.

It's easy to dismiss measures like this as "touchy-feely nonsense" that gets in the way of market forces. But you know what else gets in the way of market forces? High taxes and Big Government—and one of the main drivers of high taxes and Big Government is family breakdown. If we can take sensible steps to make work more family friendly, and thereby help keep families together, then businesses—and all of us—will be better off in the long run.

That's the thinking behind the most revolutionary change I'd like to see in America's support for families with children. It's based on a very practical, human reality of family life: the earliest time is the hardest. Surviving the birth of a new baby and the first few months of sleeplessness, stress, and disruption tests even the strongest. "About two-thirds of couples had serious problems in the first three years of the baby's life, where their happiness with one another went down. . . . Their hostility increased," observed psychologist John Gottman of his "Baby Makes Three" research program. (Having studied relationship success and failure for more than thirty years, and developed a system to predict with 94 percent accuracy the marriages that would end in divorce, Gottman aims to be to marriage what Masters and Johnson were to sex.)

"When there is a precipitous decline in relationship satisfaction and an increase in hostility, it transfers to the baby and affects the baby," Gottman told the American Psychological Association's publication *Monitor on Psychology*, citing their increased chances of later developing depression, poor social skills, and conduct disorder. The data backs up these observations: the time immediately after the birth of a child is one of the most common for couples to split up. As Gottman observed: "The baby required immediate attention. . . . It's stressful. You're not sleeping. You're irritable." If couples aren't helped through this time, they can easily believe their relationships are at fault and that they should separate.

If there's one time that it really makes sense to provide support to families, it's around when children are born and in the early years before they go to school. In most developed countries, registered nurses visit parents in the home and help new parents transition into the major life change that parenthood is. In Britain, there is a long tradition of "Health Visitors," in which nurses visit families to offer prenatal and postnatal advice and care. Covered by the National Health Service, it is free and available to families right across the socioeconomic spectrum. Rachel and I were extremely appreciative of the home visits we received when our first son was born.

For high-risk populations, these visits can literally be life savers, spotting potential signs of abuse or neglect and reducing infant mortality rates. But they can be marriage savers, too, not just helping new parents take care of their baby or growing child, but spotting signs of trouble or tension in the family and directing parents toward local community resources they could turn to for help—whether that's advice on parenting techniques, relationship counseling, keeping healthy, or just a local parents' group for mutual support. The ideal structure for this kind of home-visiting service is for a family to receive regular visits from the same person at declining frequency for the first few years after a child's birth—especially with the first child. For example, a weekly visit for the first month; once a month for the next six months; then twice a year until the child starts school. In the fragile weeks and months after birth, when exhaustion and disruption are often overwhelming, it is no small favor to receive friendly medical, psychological, and social services all delivered to your doorstep.

In an abstract, ideological sense, some might see the idea of home visiting along these lines to be a nightmare vision of the "nanny state." But when you look at it in practical, human terms, it becomes something very different. New parents are typically crying out for support and reassurance; for some families lucky enough to have relatives close by, perhaps they can provide it. But that's increasingly rare. Where government does provide a service of this kind directly, it's typically the case that the "visitor"—a trained nurse, remember—becomes one of the most trusted people for that family, a listener and assistant who can handle in a caring but professional way the most intimate aspects of everyday life as a parent.

In any case, as we've seen in other areas of policy, the actual delivery of a home-visiting service needn't be tied to the state itself. I believe strongly that we should set ourselves the aim of a Universal Home-Visiting Service for every family in America; guaranteed by the state but competitively provided by the market through for-profit and nonprofit enterprises—for example local hospitals, universities, or pediatric practices. Of course this would represent a cost to the taxpayer, but a relatively trivial one compared to the vast sums lost to fraud, waste, and overmedicalization within our grotesquely uncompetitive healthcare system (see Chapter 1). And a Universal Home-Visiting Service would yield remarkable returns to society at large. Evaluations of Nurse-Family Partnerships, a highly successful home-visiting program founded in Colorado in the 1970s and still going strong, have found enormous positive returns, including savings from the avoidance of social costs down the line such as those associated with crime or welfare dependency. But beyond dollars and cents, just think of the peace of mind we could give working families by helping make new parenthood a little easier.

2. PARENTING EDUCATION

One of the biggest social divides that has opened up between the elite and working Americans is parenting. The wealthiest and most privileged parents invest more and more time and money in their children's development and education and, as we have already seen, are more likely to be married and devoted to child-rearing as the central "project" of their lives. As a result, the elite (the top 20 percent, at least) are entrenching their advantages, pulling away from the middle and working classes and contributing to a collapse of social mobility in America. This trend has been brilliantly documented by Richard Reeves of the Brookings Institution in his book *Dream Hoarders: How the American Upper Middle Class Is Leaving Everyone Else in the Dust*.

What's the positive populist response? Not to condemn the elites for their commitment to their children's future success. Good luck to them. The right answer is to help working families give their children the best possible start in life, too. And much of that comes down to parenting. In fact, studies have shown that parenting style is the key factor in determining children's life chances, more important even than their family's economic circumstances.

The conventional wisdom about parenting is that it's one of those instinctive or inherited things that everyone knows how to do, without external advice or help (other than from a well-meaning grandmother). This is, of course, nonsense. Yes, it's true that parents have been raising children successfully for many thousands of years without help from "experts" or "busybodies" from outside the immediate family. But it's also true that the world is changing faster than ever, it's tougher and more competitive, and the skills children now need in order to navigate and succeed in it are increasingly the kind of character skills that are more dependent on what their parents do than on what their teachers do. In any case, you only have to look at the burgeoning market for parenting books and video content to see that parents want all the "expert" advice they can get. But like anything else, a book or a video gets you only so far.

The evidence shows that the best way to help parents acquire the tips and confidence they're so desperately looking for is through in-person parenting classes in the company of other parents. The most successful examples are eight-to-ten-week courses with one class a week, usually in the evenings, of about two hours. Participants extol the virtues not just of the practical hands-on confidence you get from a class, but the camaraderie with the other parents: the ability to ask questions, bounce ideas off someone, and, most important, relieve the pervasive sense of guilt and inadequacy that so many parents feel by sharing war stories and realizing they are not alone in finding parenting really, really hard. But there's a stigma attached to parenting education. Aren't parenting classes supposed to be for *failed* parents? The ones who've had their children taken away from them or had run-ins with the "system"? Why would any self-respecting parent go to one? Wouldn't that be a public admission of parental inadequacy?

These were exactly the concerns people had inside government when I first investigated this area of policy as part of David Cameron's team. Our response back then was to try to change the way parenting classes were seen. Instead of being something that was done *to* you for being a *bad* parent, we wanted it to be something you chose to do because it was part of being a good parent. Our aim was to try to make parenting education positive and aspirational. We partnered with the national pharmacy chain Boots to provide parents with information about daytime or evening courses in their area, and to distribute vouchers for those courses. The idea was to stimulate a vibrant market in parenting education, just as has happened in personal fitness over the past couple of decades, with gyms and fitness centers in every town and city helping to move personal training from something that was once the preserve of the moneyed elite to a mainstream activity (and a multibillion-dollar industry).

We need something similar in America today—and, in fact, at the time of this writing I'm planning to start a new business in this exact area. If attending a parenting course became as mainstream as going to the gym or taking driving lessons, the impact on our society would be transformational. It would help equalize opportunity, reboot social mobility, and above all, help families on a human level to deal with those anxieties that can be all-consuming: How should I discipline my kids? How do I stop siblings fighting all the time? What's the best way to limit screen time?

These questions and the hundreds like them that parents of all backgrounds in America ask every single day may sound mundane and irrelevant to a discussion of populist politics. But they are at the very heart of the Populist Society. Because if we can help parents answer these questions, and do so in a practical way, we can start to make sure that every child is raised in a stable, loving home that launches them into the world prepared to thrive and flourish, wherever they come from.

3. COMBAT TOXIC STRESS IN CHILDREN

The ideas outlined above are universal. Supporting families and marriage, home visiting, parenting education—all families can participate in and benefit from these things. But we all know that there are families in America living in much tougher conditions, with much more serious challenges than most. The stress that a typical family will experience with the arrival of a new baby is nothing compared to the stress that children live with when they grow up in troubled families and unstable homes, in neighborhoods afflicted by poverty and crime. The stress experienced by children in these circumstances can harm them for the rest of their lives. In some cases it can literally be toxic to their bodies. According to Harvard's Center on the Developing Child:

> Toxic stress response can occur when a child experiences strong, frequent, and/or prolonged adversity—such as phys-

ical or emotional abuse, chronic neglect, caregiver substance abuse or mental illness, exposure to violence, and/or the accumulated burdens of family economic hardship—without adequate adult support. This kind of prolonged activation of the stress response systems can disrupt the development of brain architecture and other organ systems, and increase the risk for stress-related disease and cognitive impairment, well into the adult years. . . . The more adverse experiences in childhood, the greater the likelihood of developmental delays and later health problems, including heart disease, diabetes, substance abuse, and depression.

Up to a fifth of American children experience mental illness in a given year; young Americans disproportionately suffer high rates of depressions, substance abuse, teen pregnancy, violence, and low college graduation rates compared to their peers in other countries. This is now a national emergency, one that wrecks individual lives and denies children the opportunity to escape the circumstances of their birth and climb the ladder of chance. You're not going to be climbing any ladders if the elevated cortisol in your brain (the natural response to the stressful experiences in your young life) makes it impossible for you to control your emotions, to concentrate in class, to work as part of a team, to trust anyone. And on top of the human cost, there is the fiscal cost: just think about the tax dollars we spend dealing with the consequences of this early failure—the cost in the criminal justice system, the welfare system, the health-care system. Doesn't it make sense to try to avoid those costs—and save those wasted lives—by intervening early to combat the effects of toxic stress and adverse childhood experience?

It needn't even cost more money at the start. Today we spend untold billions of dollars on an uncoordinated patchwork of social services provided by multiple agencies that dehumanize and confuse the families they're trying to help. I've heard the same story over and over again, in city after city: endless well-meaning "interventions" targeting the same small number of families, expecting them to show up for appointments with fourteen or fifteen different agencies, sometimes working at cross-purposes, where people inevitably turn into case numbers. Imagine if we could replace today's bureaucratic mess with one trusted professional whose sole focus is a troubled family, who could observe the environment a child is experiencing and work to end the dysfunction.

In my view, this effort should be organized like a military campaign. In every major city in America, identify the relatively small number of families who have the most problems and who cause the most problems (they're usually the same). Assign each of them a trained family worker whose starting point should be to study how the family's problems are interconnected: unemployment, debt, substance abuse, violence, educational failure. Then give the family workers the responsibility and discretion to respond creatively to the very different human circumstances they encounter. Stop all the other interventions: give the family worker the power to determine what the family needs.

Over the past few years, I've gotten to know Dr. Nadine Burke Harris, an inspiring pediatrician who set up her clinic in the poorest, toughest neighborhood in San Francisco in order to work on these types of problems. She is one of America's leading advocates on toxic stress and is the author of *The Deepest Well—Healing the Long-Term Effects of Childhood Adversity*. She argues persuasively that one of the first things we need to do is identify which children are most in need of help, by incorporating a simple test for ACEs (Adverse Childhood Experiences) into regular pediatric checkups. Beyond that, we need to make everyone—from parents and teachers to relatives—aware of the harmful effects of toxic stress on children so that they, too, can help identify it. Families won't be able to magically end domestic disputes or move out of crime-infested neighborhoods, but even minor steps in the right direction, like helping children get more sleep or helping parents shield their children from their arguments, can make a big difference.

For community members who often interact with children, like doctors, teachers, coaches, and clergy, understanding the causes and effects of toxic stress could lead to different approaches to discipline and treatment, or even proactive steps to alleviate difficult home environments they recognize. Children with toxic stress often act out, misbehave, or fall victim to addiction themselves. Creating strategies and protocols to address toxic stress in communities where it is common would help save countless young people from going down self-destructive paths.

If Positive Populism is all about people power, that power can't be narrowly defined in a purely political or administrative sense. Real power is about having the ability to shape your own destiny, and what happens in your family is one of the most crucial factors—perhaps the most crucial. We can't wave a wand and turn every family in America into a neatly ordered template of the ideal—nor should we try. But families do deserve more than platitudes. It's not good enough to simply lament the decline of the family and yearn for a mythical golden age (that in any case was not nearly as great as some may fondly imagine). As we've seen in this chapter, there are specific, practical steps we can take to support families, and to do all we can to make sure every child is raised in a stable, loving home.

EQUALLY, WE MUST NOT ASSUME that we can organize these interventions from on high in some sweeping, centralized act of bureaucratic zeal. Yes, we can specify overall aims; establish standards and expectations, provide funding. To those who say we can't afford to spend money supporting America's families, there are two answers: first that such support will save money by cutting the costs of social failure, and second that it is surely a better use of our resources than almost everything else government spends money on today—especially the trillions wasted on corrupt contracts with the military industrial complex for spurious interventions overseas. But regardless of how much we spend, the best solutions will be the local and the personal, those that are rooted in the community. Let's unleash them, with the goal of making America the best place in the world to start and raise a family. That would be a tremendous start in helping to repair our torn social fabric.

IN A NUTSHELL . . .

Strong families are a vital part of Positive Populism. But that doesn't mean preaching about family values; it means practical action to turn around the deeply damaging and decades-long trend of family breakdown. We need to value families, respect them, and give them the infrastructure they need to flourish:

1. Actively support marriage and families: Government shouldn't be neutral when it comes to marriage; it should support stable, two-parent households by stopping the marriage penalty in the welfare system, improving paid parental leave (for mothers and fathers), and implementing a Universal Home-Visiting Service, whereby nurses would come and offer counsel to new parents.

2. Parenting education: Parenting isn't easy; we should help all new parents learn the basic skills they need by making parenting classes an aspirational social norm.

3. Combat toxic stress in children: Children who grow up in families that are in crisis are likely to suffer from the ill effects of toxic stress, permanently harming their cognitive development. We should equip specialized highly trained family workers with the authority to help those families—and those children—get back on track.

5

COMMUNITY

MY TIME WORKING at 10 Downing Street earned me some unwanted attention in the British tabloids, and even a fleeting encounter with pop culture fame: a bald-headed, casually dressed character spouting new-age public relations gobbledygook on a BBC political sitcom (literally *Veep*'s precursor) was modeled after me. People were oddly fascinated by my habit of walking around the office wearing socks but no shoes. I thought it was perfectly normal—the inside of 10 Downing Street is like a posh aristocratic home, full of antique furnishings and plush carpets. And yet it seemed almost impossible to read a newspaper article about me that didn't at some point include the phrase "padding around No. 10 in his stockinged feet." Padding? Stockinged? Whatever. But perhaps nothing arched more eyebrows among Westminster's elite than the one policy idea of the Cameron administration that became most associated with me: the argument that we should aim for a "Big Society, not Big Government."

That's because from a Conservative leader who had grown up

under Prime Minister Margaret Thatcher, such an acknowledgment of the importance of community came as a complete shock. You see, Thatcher's most famous statement on society was a pointed disavowal of its existence. "They are casting their problems at society," she said in an interview in 1987, at the height of her powers as prime minister. "And as you know, there's no such thing as society. There are individual men and women and families."

"There's no such thing as society." It became the most famous phrase she ever uttered, used by her critics to characterize Thatcherism as a cruel and selfish ideology. Although, as is evident from the full quote, "Maggie" intended something more positive (that individuals and families are the true building blocks of society), the reason the phrase stuck was that it did capture something of the spirit of Thatcherism, which argued that rugged individualism, not community solidarity, would renew the country after the unmitigated disaster inflicted on Britons in the 1960s and '70s by the previous Labour government's socialist policies. (And when I say socialist, I mean full-on socialist: 98 percent top rate of tax, nationalization, state-controlled enterprises, the whole deal. They made Bernie Sanders look like Rand Paul by comparison.) Margaret Thatcher's policy agenda was an essential correction: it saved Britain from seemingly terminal decline. But it was based on a conviction that prioritized the individual, a conviction that I understood most deeply in a profoundly moving personal moment with the Iron Lady.

When she reached the milestone of her eightieth birthday in 2005, a number of celebrations, some public, some private, were organized by her friends and supporters. I had the enormous honor of being invited to one of the most intimate: a dinner at the Carlton Club (the traditional home of the British Conservative Party) hosted by then party leader Michael Howard; my wife, Rachel, was at that time his senior advisor. There were just twelve of us around the table, and I was seated next but one to the former prime minister. She looked magnificent: impeccably, even regally dressed and with that famous hair as perfectly coiffed as ever. But in advance of the dinner we had all been warned that her mind had been much diminished as a result of rapidly advancing dementia and a series of minor strokes. We were asked to be prepared for the possibility that she would not recognize anyone. We were not to be fazed by any rambling conversation or long pauses. She would acknowledge her celebratory toast but not actually speak herself.

At the event, it didn't quite work out like that. After Howard paid her a glowing tribute, Lady Thatcher slowly got to her feet. She was, it seemed, intending to speak after all. The glances around the table showed that nobody thought this was a good idea. There was an uncomfortably long pause. Our hearts were in our mouths; the last thing anyone wanted was to see her humiliated. But then something rather miraculous happened. She started speaking, incredibly clearly and articulately. She spoke for about five minutes, and it was about as pure an encapsulation of her political philosophy as you could ask for. It was word perfect, lucid, and utterly transfixing. Honestly, it was one of the most moving things I have ever witnessed. This extraordinary, brave woman, her once all-conquering powers snatched from her by illness, forcing nature to bend to her will for those five minutes so she could once again inspire people with the vision she fought for throughout her life.

And what was that vision? I'll never forget the words she used that night to sum it all up, a phrase that Americans will readily recognize: "Liberty Under the Law." That's what it had all been about, she told us. "Liberty Under the Law." She believed passionately that if you set people free, they will do the right thing and all will benefit. The individual was not just to be liberated but venerated; collective action was either an afterthought or dismissed. This powerful conviction informed the drive of 1980s conservatism toward cutting government and the public sector anywhere and everywhere possible. The Reagan Revolution was of course based on a similar philosophical foundation. No wonder the two leaders were such political soul mates.

Looking back on those days, it is absolutely clear that government needed to be cut back. The economic dynamism seen in both the United States and the United Kingdom in response to pro-market reforms was evidence of the galvanizing power of an individualist ideology. Growth rates soared after the sluggish 1970s. Perhaps the ultimate tribute was paid by the opposition parties on both sides of the Atlantic: Bill Clinton here and Tony Blair over there both conceded intellectual defeat, moved their parties to the right, and embraced the role of markets and deregulation—in rhetorical terms at least.

But it seems clear now that something important was also lost in those years, and the decades that followed, in Britain certainly but even more so here in America. Not just a loss of economic security for working people, as we saw in Chapter 1, but something that affects everyone. You hear it everywhere today: *We've lost our sense of community.* There is a widespread and uneasy awareness of social breakdown as devastating as the family breakdown described in Chapter 4. More and more people describe a feeling of isolation and atomization, despite (or even, partly, because of?) the technological tools that purport to bring us together. Social trust has broken down, whether that's in the institutions that are supposed to make society work, between the groups we belong to and share our culture with, or simply in each other. Our social fabric is torn, and that's what led David Cameron, in a deliberately provocative phrase, to engage in a retrospective debate with Margaret Thatcher: "There is such a thing as society," he said, "it's just not the same thing as the state." This belief in the importance of community informed the argument that I helped craft into a phrase that, for better or worse, became the one I'm most remembered for in Britain: "Big Society, not Big Government."

Here in America today, there is an even more urgent need to strengthen community bonds, especially at the local level. Over many decades now, those bonds have been carelessly torn apart by elitists who disdain local community in favor of more abstract or class-based forms of collective association. A weekend house party in the Hamptons, rather than coffee and donuts with friends and neighbors after church. Skiing in Aspen rather than a local running club. Elites find it hard to understand or even care about local community because their outlook is typically global, disconnected from their immediate surroundings. But for most Americans, community is precisely where life takes on meaning, through friendship, responsibility, and service.

At the time that I was developing a specific set of policy ideas to strengthen communities in the United Kingdom, I came across a column in the *New York Times* that perfectly articulated the American version of my thesis:

> Republicans are so much the party of individualism and freedom these days that they are no longer the party of community and order. This puts them out of touch with the young, who are exceptionally community-oriented. It gives them nothing to say to the lower middle class, who fear that capitalism has gone haywire. It gives them little to say to the upper middle class, who are interested in the environment and other common concerns.

The column was by David Brooks. He mused whether Americans (particularly Republicans) love western movies because the genre celebrates rugged individualism. Or because westerns like the kind that director John Ford made celebrated the interconnectedness of those early adventurers, who worked together to create communities from scratch: building churches and schoolhouses, recruiting teachers, preachers, doctors, and entertainment.

In many ways, building and sustaining community is the essential American virtue, demonstrated consistently since the nation's founding—from the earliest settlers to the colonists to the pioneers who conquered the West. And community is not just an accident of geographical colocation. It is the result of the conscious and intricate construction of informal and formal institutions: the church, the sports club, the local charity. These provide the ongoing reason for individuals and families to connect with each other, to support each other, to help each other in hard times. We rightly celebrate "self-reliance" in America as an essential bulwark against government overreach. But in practice, self-reliance doesn't mean relying on no one but yourself. It means relying on one another rather than the government. Self-reliance is really about community.

Over the past few decades, elitist attitudes and policies have led to a sustained and destructive assault on the building blocks of community. These attitudes and policies can be defined by one word: *centralization*. As control over, and responsibility for, more and more aspects of daily life has slipped from the hands of local communities and into the hands of distant decision makers, it makes less and less sense for people to associate locally. You see this in many ways, from decisions about local zoning and the physical planning of neighborhoods, to the centralization of the economy, with globalization and complex webs of corporate ownership and control destroying local businesses that once played not just an economic role, but a vital civic role, too. Free market ideology— driven by the financial and business elite and implemented by their servants in both the Republican and Democratic parties—put the needs of big business ahead of all other considerations. As we saw in Chapter 3, the only thing that was allowed to matter was "consumer welfare."

But "consumers" are people, too. Their welfare means more to them than price. It means a neighborhood that's still distinctive, rather than one that looks like every other neighborhood because the giant global corporations that have colonized it find it more "efficient" to offer the exact same thing in the exact same way, everywhere.

Consumers are members of communities. Their welfare includes the sense of trust that comes when the local employer is run by people who are actually local, rather than by a boss halfway round the world. From both the cultural left and the corporate right, community in America suffered body blow after body blow from the 1970s onward. The social fabric frayed as people moved away from organized religion, private sector labor unions and trade associations, and close-knit neighborhoods that provided "eyes on the street," in the words of the legendary urbanist and community advocate Jane Jacobs.

Repairing our torn social fabric is a central aim of Positive Populism, and restoring community life is at the heart of that effort. Partly that is about reversing the centralization of the economy, along the lines set out in Chapter 3. And partly it is about reversing the centralization of government—the theme of Chapter 7. But there is also direct and positive work we can do within communities. In order to rebuild them, we shouldn't just bemoan the fact that "there's so little community spirit these days." We can invent new ways—real, tangible ways—for people to come together at the community level. We can create a new civic infrastructure in which to participate.

Frankly, policy makers on both sides of the aisle have spent far too little time thinking about such practical aspects of social policy. Liberals have tended to equate the idea of community either with identity (an exclusionary interpretation), or with government itself (whose overreach and centralization have been a big part of the reason communities have withered). Conservatives, for their part, have underestimated the proactive work required to build and sustain community, as if all that has to happen for community to flourish is for government to get out of the way. If only it were that simple. The truth is, we have to work hard to re-create in our modern age the community foundations that economic, social, and technological "progress" have washed away. So here are three practical ideas to revolutionize community in America.

It starts with the neighborhood.

1. ALL POWER TO THE NEIGHBORHOOD!

There was a time when a community was easy to spot: it looked like membership in a church. Or labor union. Or a business association united by brick-and-mortar concerns. But today our notion of community is more likely to be understood in terms of sprawling online social networks that actively take people away from their local community. A 2016 Nielsen report found that adults spend 10 hours and 39 minutes a day consuming online media. Some say that time spent interacting with others through technology is simply a modern form of community, no worse than previous incarnations: Who are we to judge?

Well, Robert Putnam's book *Bowling Alone: The Collapse and Revival of American Community* used the decline of bowling leagues to make a sobering point about the deterioration of social capital. First published in 2000, *Bowling Alone* could not predict that online communities in which people have hundreds, even thousands, of "friends" and "followers" would replace real-life interaction to the degree it has today. Those online "communities" are illusory at best. Despite sharing broad affinities, we can't possibly have a meaningful relationship with many thousands of people; we're just not wired for it. In a study of British families' Christmas card lists around the same time *Bowling Alone* was published, evolutionary psychologist Robin Dunbar found that the number conducive to the strongest communal bonding is 150 people, on average (although our brains can recognize ten times as many faces). That figure—150—has since become known as "Dunbar's number," and whether it's Christmas card lists, hunter-gatherer tribes, or military units, apparently we are neurologically limited when it comes to genuine human relationships.

You could make endless lists of 150-people groupings—and perhaps we ought to create and join more of them to advocate on particular issues we care about. But for the general concerns of our day-to-day lives, the number 150 roughly maps onto the community where much of our lives are based: our neighborhoods. In an ideal world designed around actual human realities, the neighborhood would therefore be the best and most basic level of civic organization. Just imagine what might be the outcome if everyone actually had a good reason to connect meaningfully with the people who are literally closest to them—the people in their neighborhood.

Can we stimulate neighborhood interaction? In certain respects, technology can make that kind of local community building easier, as anyone who has belonged to a neighborhood Listserv or used the neighborhood social network NextDoor.com can attest. Advances in civil engineering and data can give us more and better information about how our local areas actually work (or don't), helping us better understand how we relate to everything from traffic patterns to pollution. In these and other ways, we have more power than ever to take collective action on the issues that most concern us at the ultralocal level.

But people are only going to take advantage of these opportunities if there's a good reason to. It's no use just exhorting people to "get involved" in their communities. People are busy. They have jobs to do, families to raise, lives to live. They will only participate in community activity if they actually get something out of it. That doesn't have to be something financial, or even something tangible. Often, a heightened feeling of control and sovereignty is enough—because one of the defining features of our age is people's loss of control: the sense that the decisions affecting their lives are made somewhere else by someone else. Neighborhood action can provide a strong counterweight to that. One mechanism we can use is a type of organization that sounds wonky and rather grand in scale, but could actually make a real impact at the local level: public-private partnerships. Public-private partnerships can take many forms, but at their core, they involve cooperation between different entities—citizens, business, government, and civic groups—with each contributing what they do best. Here are two possible models to follow.

As part of her drive to break up a monolithic and bloated public sector, Margaret Thatcher in the 1980s introduced "Compulsory Competitive Tendering" for local government services. Basically, local councils were required to put their services out to competitive bid, inviting outsiders to show how they could run waste collection, libraries, and so on at higher quality for less taxpayer money. The left saw it as an attack on public-sector unions; the right claimed it made local services more efficient. But neither side made the really important point: that for many services, the policy was operating in far too centralizing a way. Whether your neighborhood park or library is run by a distant corporation or a distant local government, it's still not run by you, the people who actually use it. Local services like these are often the lifeblood of a community: so why can't the community itself be invited to run them? Of course, that doesn't fit with the elitist spreadsheet-driven organizational orthodoxy of our bureaucratized and management consultant–obsessed modern age. But isn't that orthodoxy exactly what we need to escape?

Let's imagine a reform that gives American neighborhoods who want it real control of the things that matter to them. You could call it "Compulsory Community Tendering." State and local governments would identify every single community- and neighborhood-based service that serves that neighborhood only. A local park, community center, or library are all good examples. (We're not talking here about a bus service that operates across a whole town or refuse collection for an entire city.) Neighborhood associations would then be given the "right to run" any or all of the services designated as neighborhood based. Local governments would be required to consider all expressions of interest and conduct an open bidding process. Budgets would be transferred from local government to local community; real empowerment and engagement would follow.

Critics might object that in such circumstances, neighborhood groups who won power over their local services would not literally want to run them, but simply set the overall direction and strategy, subcontracting the actual operations to a private- or public-sector provider. In which case: What has really changed? And it's true that the outsourcing trends of the last few decades have led to the emergence of giant global service corporations that hoover up local government contracts in a way that leads to more centralization, not less. But there are a number of ways we can guard against this.

First, if we get tough about antitrust, as described in Chapter 3, we will hamper the ability of companies to grow to a size where they dominate a market in negative ways. Second, if we reform the rotten and corrupt system of public sector procurement, as set out in Chapter 8, we can make it much easier for new entrants and small, local contractors to bid for and win contracts at any level of government. But finally, don't discount the possibility that some neighborhoods might actually want to run their local services locally, setting up community-owned businesses or cooperatives that employ local people and keep assets and resources within the community.

Imagine what the results of Compulsory Community Tendering could be if it was implemented by state and local governments right across the country, in a place as civic-minded as America. "There's this long tradition of commitment to ideals that binds Americans together," says Robin Dunbar. "That isn't always true elsewhere. In a way, Americans are lucky in that respect."

My hunch is that he's right. But we need to create the civic infrastructure that will give people a good reason to come together. Voluntary people power, resulting from organic community building, would alleviate many of the ailments that Big Government seeks to fix but can't. Government can help get it going by making it easier for community groups to organize and take legal responsibility for the local services that matter to them. Neighborhood power is a big part of the Populist Society.

2. CIVIC SERVICE

It's one thing to give neighborhood associations the power to take control of local services. It's great when it works, but it's quite the commitment, and not for everyone. Is there a lower-impact way to engage people in their neighborhoods and start to rebuild local community through boosting personal interactions? A new way of doing this occurred to me after I visited, of all places, a neighborhood grocery store a few years ago.

Situated in Brooklyn (yes, I know, but bear with me . . .), the Park Slope Food Co-op is a membership-only grocery store that features local, sustainable food at a huge discount—from 20 to 40 percent. The only catch? You have to be a member to shop there, and membership isn't free. Yes, there's a small fee, but the real member contribution is labor—two hours forty-five minutes every four weeks, or thirteen times per year. Members contribute their time, and in return have access to great food at much lower prices. (It works because labor costs are a disproportionately large expense for a small retail store.)

When a friend of mine first took me to see the co-op, I almost laughed out loud; it comes dangerously close to self-parody. But then I saw its real value. The Park Slope Food Co-op isn't a grocery store; it's a community. Its members might come for the affordable produce, but they stay because they've become friends with the "squads" they work with each month, enjoy attending the co-op's social events, and value having something concrete and useful to do alongside their neighbors. Through its light but tightly structured system for community participation (just under three hours a month) a grocery store has turned into a real neighborhood center, the local hub for everything from movie nights to financial advice to parent support groups.

What can this grocery store teach us about civic participation? It shows that if you create the structure for people to come together in their neighborhood, and an incentive for doing so, they will. People are happy to give their time and work alongside others— especially if they're going to directly see the benefits of their work, such as lower shopping bills.

This isn't a new concept, after all. Just think of all the activities you might volunteer for as a parent: PTA, classroom helper, soccer coach. Businesses find that their employees enjoy organized community volunteering, especially the camaraderie that comes with it. But it does have to be organized—it doesn't just spring up on its own. Now think of all the people who may not come across these organized opportunities to get involved locally—people who don't have children in school, or who aren't working. All they need is a little push. And technology is making it easier. In Estonia, three tech entrepreneurs created software based on Google Earth to map and take pictures of more than three thousand illegal garbage dumps around the country. Using their new maps and social media, they mobilized fifty thousand people—some 4 percent of the country's population—to get together to clean up littered forests one weekend in May 2008. The event was so successful that it evolved into a global campaign with millions of participants. If you give people the tools, they'll tutor kids, clean beaches, plant trees, paint schools, and more; it's no cliché to say they'll change the world.

But impact, however important, is only half the value that this kind of neighborhood participation brings. Just as important a benefit is the commonwealth created. And I mean that in the literal sense of the word. By contributing to the common good, participants feel more invested in their communities—and will become more actively involved in their upkeep. Maybe they'll get involved in other local campaigns, or take an interest in whether to put in that new public swimming pool. The bottom line is that they'll have a renewed faith in society—in democracy—and be more active citizens in all aspects of their lives.

So let's create more Park Slope Food Co-ops. Not actual co-ops, necessarily, but community-based service organizations. What a great model for bringing people into the civic sphere. We could help strengthen a neighborhood's social fabric by creating something called "Civic Service." It could be a little like jury duty, except more predictable and regular. Let's identify useful roles in communities that local residents could fill and then invite—or, in the famous phrase of the behavioral economists, "nudge" them though incentives like discounts on local taxes—to give two or three hours of service a month, just like the members of the Park Slope Food Co-op. It would help people connect with their neighbors and increase their sense of belonging and social responsibility. The aim shouldn't be to force or cajole anyone, but to create an expectation, a new norm of civic participation.

And we should start early.

3. AMERICAN CITIZEN SERVICE

One of the most pessimistic trends today is that young people seem to be growing up without knowing what it's like to be part of a real offline community. Occasionally you'll see an upswing of interest in and support for a cause that is in the news. But the overall numbers tell a less positive story: compared to previous generations, young people leave the house less, see their friends less, join civic groups less. It was a similar picture in Britain when I was investigating the causes of and potential solutions to social breakdown there—and that's why I think one of the most valuable contributions I made while working in government was the creation of National Citizen Service (NCS), a program for young people between the ages of fifteen and seventeen.

Unlike its somewhat martial-sounding name, National Citizen Service has nothing whatsoever to do with the military, and unlike the mandatory service in countries like Singapore, Finland, or Israel, it is entirely voluntary. But it was inspired by the idea of creating a nonmilitary form of national service, something that would bring everyone together in a common effort. If you speak to

British people who took part in and remember National Service, as the military draft was known in the United Kingdom, they all say the same thing: there may have been aspects of it that they hated at the time but the one thing they loved was that it was something "we all did together." It literally brought the country together—people from every different background and part of the nation working alongside each other in a common endeavor. Our aim in creating National Citizen Service was to build that same sense of social cohesion in today's generation of young people.

In designing and then implementing the program, we were highly aware of all the myriad organizations, some small and local, others large and national, that offered opportunities for young people to serve their communities. We worked with them and learned from them, and wanted them to be part of the new effort we were creating. The big difference between what we were proposing and what was already on offer was its universality: we truly wanted something that literally every teenager in the United Kingdom would participate in around the time of their sixteenth birthday. A shared "rite of passage" that would help bring the country together through a common experience.

One of the core elements of the NCS program is community service. The participating teens are challenged to focus on how they can improve their own communities. Participants live away from home (perhaps for the first time in their lives) for two weeks over the summer—the first week spent in an Outward Bound–style camp where they take part in pretty grueling outdoor activities through which they learn confidence and social skills, and the second in a university environment run by head teachers. When the two weeks away come to a close, the students return to their homes prepared to work on a community service program of their own choosing and dedicate thirty hours toward its implementation. This might include spending time with the elderly, raising money for local charities or homeless shelters, or renovating public spaces. NCS graduates list their status on their resumes and college applications, and it's a mark of distinction that employers are starting to recognize.

While it is backed by government, NCS is mostly run through partnerships with private-sector and nonprofit partners such as charities, college consortia, and businesses who have an interest in developing the nation's talent pipeline. As a result, the cost to each student's family is approximately $65—for the whole program, including room and board. Since its 2010 pilot program, it has already graduated 200,000 students, and its goal is one million by 2020.

The skills cultivated at NCS are the same kind of skills that Britain's elite cultivate by sending their children to boarding school and then to university. I was lucky enough to get those life-changing experiences, too, at Christ's Hospital and then Oxford. But for the majority of British students—and I'd venture to guess the majority of American students—NCS fills an incomparable void.

Beyond helping to level the playing field and imbuing young people with an ethos of service, NCS does something else that's vital: it breaks down social barriers by mixing participants from vastly different social, ethnic, and class backgrounds. This is a crucial element of the design of the program, and one of the reasons I insisted on the residential component. I wanted to take young people out of their familiar settings and introduce them to the kind of people they had never met before: people from different parts of the country, different ethnic backgrounds, and, perhaps most important, different economic classes.

I think something like this could make a huge contribution to repairing America's torn social fabric. The last time young Americans had a common solidarity-building generational experience, we were fighting a world war. The Americans who fought together in World War II came back with a common understanding of what it meant to be American because they experienced a much fuller range of *who* could be an American.

What is there that brings the entire American community together today? Of course there are many thousands of fantastic service programs of many different kinds for young people right across the country. But nothing that "we all do together." Nothing that includes the kind of social mixing that can help break down the barriers of mistrust and suspicion that seem to be getting higher all the time. American Citizen Service designed for the twenty-first century would help mobilize the same spirit of unity that infused the nation postwar—but without the tragedy of a global conflagration, and without excluding any part of our national community.

If we want people to play an active role in their communities, we have to prepare them. By making service a formative, enjoyable experience, and vitally, a universally shared one, American Citizen Service would go a long way toward preparing young people for a lifetime of civic engagement. Combined with the other ideas in this chapter for strengthening neighborhoods and local communities—and the revolutionary ideas in Chapter 7 for localism and decentralizing government, it could help bring our sadly fractured country together.

IN A NUTSHELL . . .

America's special brand of self-reliance will only survive if we remember that it depends on community. But America's social fabric is torn and we need to take active steps to repair it and reinvigorate our shared democratic spirit. Let's put community front and center of our lives again.

1. **All power to the neighborhood:** Make the communities where we live the basic unit of civic interaction; let's use Compulsory Community Tendering to give neighborhoods a tangible, practical reason to come together.

2. **Civic Service:** Identify useful roles that community members can carry out in the neighborhood on a regular basis and give them incentives to do so, bringing us closer together through practical action.

3. **American Citizen Service:** Create a common national service program that every teenager in America goes through around the summer of their sixteenth year, teaching valuable life skills and lessons, breaking down socioeconomic barriers, and creating a generational *esprit de corps*.

6

COUNTRY

FAMILY, COMMUNITY—THEN COUNTRY: the nation-state is the third indispensable part of our social fabric, and a key component of our conception of the Populist Society. This is not, as we shall see, for the kind of tribal, nationalistic reasons that elitist critics of populism like to claim. The nation-state is indispensable to our social fabric because it's where we resolve our inevitable differences, legitimately and democratically. A country can do that in a way that an international, multilateral organization can never accomplish.

It's *E Pluribus Unum,* not *E Pluribus UN.*

Moreover, there is something particularly positive about America's interpretation of the nation-state, and I feel it very personally. I know all about tribalism: my Hungarian ancestors, the Magyars, were literally a tribe that moved across Asia into Europe and settled there a thousand or so years ago. Magyarorszag—Magyar Country, as the Hungarians call it—is still a pretty tribal place today, ethnically homogeneous and acutely conscious of its historic victimhood and current isolation in a part of the world dominated by Slavs, with whom Hungarians are frequently (and infuriatingly, from their point of view) lumped together. I know all about nationalism, too: when I was growing up in the United Kingdom, the symbols of British nationhood—the Union Jack flag, the national anthem, "Rule Britannia"—had been captured and besmirched by skinheads and the racist far right. In contrast, what I always admired about America (and what I appreciate with much greater understanding now that my home is here) is the way that the American nation-state represents not a tribal identity or the accumulations of history, but a positive idea, open to all who sign up to its precepts. That's why I love seeing the Stars and Stripes proudly displayed and hearing "The Star-Spangled Banner" sung at sporting events. And it's why I'm sad to see that America's unashamed and widely shared patriotism seems today to be under assault.

We've stopped believing in the powerful national story that once brought America together: the story of equal opportunity. The land of the free and the home of the brave. One nation, under God, indivisible, with liberty and justice for all. These words are so powerful—and yet they ring so hollow for so many Americans today. A central aim of the Populist Society must surely be to renew that national story in a way that is both inspiring and believable for every citizen. That can partly be achieved through rebuilding community, as described in the previous chapter—especially with American Citizen Service. But it also requires us to stop denigrating the very notion of the nation-state.

For those Americans whose experience and history in this nation is one of subjugation and discrimination, you can understand why an exhortation to embrace patriotism is a bitter pill to swallow. For the so-called enlightened elites, on the other hand, their rejection of patriotism is not because they have suffered at America's hands, but for precisely the opposite reason. Their prosperity and progress, as they see it, has elevated them above the humdrum concerns of nation. The world is now their oyster, and patriotism is for other people. They are *global* citizens, don't you know. The little people who are "proud to be an American"—well, they're self-evidently guilty of tribalism, nationalism, racism, nativism, or just plain bigotry.

But country matters deeply. It forms the basis of our identity. What an Arizonan, an Alabaman, and an Alaskan all share is that they are Americans, and hold common values as a result. If the state is a country's body, the nation is its soul. And in a democracy, the nation only functions when there is a sense of solidarity among its people—in good times and in bad. America endured the Great Depression and celebrated putting a man on the moon; Britain survived the Blitz and built the National Health Service. Nations are not immutable, but they are forged in time and place—and democracy only works *because* they have definition.

Exactly how they are defined, though, is ultimately up to their citizens (or at least, should be). Whether or not *we the people* have the capacity to absorb more immigrants and using which criteria; with which kind of countries *we the people* would like to trade; which military interventions *we the people* are willing to die for . . . these are questions that can only be decided by a defined country, with borders and rules and, crucially, voters.

International elites living in New York, San Francisco, Washington, London, Paris, and Brussels pretend to be democratic, but over time, they've started identifying with each other more easily than they do with their fellow countrymen. They've become a class unto themselves, insensitive to the feelings of working people who are enfranchised not by their wealth or clout or multiple passports, but by their democratic right to cast a vote. As a member of the elite now, I know what I'm talking about. I myself have ties to several different countries. I grew up spending summers visiting my family in Hungary, and all my living relatives, apart from my mother, are still there. My wife and our children were able to move from London to California for amazing career opportunities and California's legendary lifestyle with ease. Aside from the occasional culture shock (do we really need that much ice?), we feel right at home. After all, in the world of the elite, the where matters far less than the who. Whether you're in New York, Washington, Aspen, or Newport, the same people move in the same circles—professional and social. Elites move blithely across borders. Yes, "globalism"—the idea that countries don't really matter anymore—has also benefited the professional class who have gained access to international education, foreign vacations, and novel cuisines. But let's be honest: it's a system designed by the elites and, unsurprisingly, it serves them very well.

The elitists' globalist mind-set was perfectly captured by British philosopher Roger Scruton in his 2017 *Wall Street Journal* essay, "The Case for Nations": "Urban elites build trust through career moves, joint projects and cooperation across borders. Like the aristocrats of old, they often form networks without reference to national boundaries. They do not, on the whole, depend upon a particular place, a particular faith or a particular routine for their sense of membership. . . ."

But regular working people do. Their first line of defense is not their lawyer or accountant; it's their rights as citizens secured by a particular nation—with its unique set of rules and protections that they can vote for or against. It is through their national governments that they express their general will, and through their country's success that they ultimately prosper. Advocates of globalism sincerely believe that theirs is the better path. It's not quite John Lennon ("Imagine there's no countries / It isn't hard to do") but it's not far off. When you start to interrogate all this, however, you quickly realize what lies behind the globalists' rather self-satisfied moral superiority. Take one of the purest statements of the globalist creed, which was delivered by Facebook CEO Mark Zuckerberg as part of his Harvard commencement address in 2017:

> The forces of freedom, openness and global community are up against the forces of authoritarianism, isolationism and nationalism. . . . The forces for the flow of knowledge, trade and immigration against those who would slow them down. This is not a battle of nations; this is a battle of ideas.

It sounds aspirational and even innocent enough. But once you start to examine it, something more insidious emerges. Who or what is this "global community" Zuckerberg speaks of? How is it accountable, and to whom? What is Zuckerberg's mandate, exactly, for privileging the global over the national? In other words, why is it right that unelected, undemocratic governance should supersede the elected, democratic kind? You kind of get the feeling that what Zuckerberg is really arguing for here is nothing more (or less) than a world run according to the things that he and his fellow Bay Area billionaires believe in.

The elites in the media and the ivory tower would have us think that allegiance to a nation-state necessarily means being bigoted and xenophobic. That's why they keep talking about "nationalism" as a threat, to be resisted. But they never explain the basis on which any national leader could possibly be justified in doing anything *other* than putting their own nation's and their own people's interests first. Is that nationalism? Or simply a functioning democracy? The globalist demand is for national leaders to demote the interests of their country and their people in pursuit of . . . what? The global interest? Who decides what that is? Oh wait—the globalists do. You might call that oligarchy, and you'd be right.

Positive populists embrace a patriotism that celebrates their own country and harnesses its power for positive ends. Yes, these ends should primarily benefit people at home, but they're not motivated in the slightest degree by a desire to disadvantage people elsewhere. You needn't put down other countries to put yours ahead. The big point is: citizenship means something. It's the pinnacle of an intricately designed system of governance that the framers of the Constitution ensured means more to American citizens than most. American patriotism is a positive and inimitable phenomenon. But it's not just the flag. It's not just the anthem. It requires sovereignty for and accountability to citizens, and the rejection of any argument or ideology that would place power in the hands of any organization or group that American citizens cannot control with their votes.

The consolidation of the global economy in the past few decades has driven an equivalent consolidation in governance. After all, nation-states are a footling inconvenience to the global corporations who crave a world where they can operate everywhere without constraint. But nobody ever cast a vote for Goldman Sachs or Google. We need to take power out of the hands of the arrogant and unaccountable globalist elite and put it back in the hands of the people, in the form of democratic nation-states. International bodies cannot, by definition, be democratic. As Roger Scruton wrote, "Democratic politics requires a *demos*. Democracy means rule by the people and requires us to know who the people are, what unites them and how they can form a government."

1. IMMIGRATION AND SOCIAL COHESION

From my earliest days in British politics, I counted myself a "Euroskeptic" precisely for these reasons. What does the general will of Britons matter to civil servants in Brussels, whom no citizen can ever vote for or against? Great Britain was the only economy in Europe to experience contracting wages and increasing GDP between 2007 and 2015, the *Financial Times* notes; but why should Brussels care about that inconvenient truth if average Britons can't vote them out of office?

Of course, the wealthy British elite, mainly Londoners with ties to its financial sector, were eager to simplify their business transactions with the rest of Europe, enjoy weekends in Spain without passports, entertain job opportunities in other capitals, and dream of retirement in Provence while collecting their British pensions. But for the average British citizen, the undoubted travel and trade upsides of European Union membership were offset by being constantly told that the EU, not the government they elected, was behind many of the important decisions that affected their lives. "Sorry, EU rules," was a constant, maddening refrain.

Hungarians—who voted to join the European Union in 2003, forty years after the United Kingdom did—learned this in an extremely painful way during the 2015 refugee crisis. It was prompted by German chancellor Angela Merkel, who without warning invited anyone fleeing conflict in Syria or the rest of the Middle East to seek refuge in Germany. Hungary became the main crossing point into Europe for migrants from the Mediterranean attracted by Merkel's offer and saw more asylum applications in proportion to population than any other EU state—second in total only to Germany itself.

But Hungary is a former communist country, exploited for decades by the Soviet Union. It simply doesn't have the wealth and infrastructure of Germany. It was in no position to absorb the number of refugees that Brussels insisted it take. Perhaps it could accommodate some; but rather than make that determination itself, its "quota" (yes, that's the term they use) was imposed on it by the European Union. My anguished cousins in the southern city of Szeged, right on the border crossing, described the chaos to me. Understandably desperate people—many of whom were not Syrian war refugees, but economic migrants (one detained by Hungarian police was a Pakistani wanted for seventy murders in his native country) were stealing fruit and vegetables from people's gardens, urinating and defecating on the streets of this beautiful university city, clogging public services, waiting for European Union registration and the shelter that they thought was their due. "Is Hungary the EU's First Rogue State?" headlines blared, after Hungarian police used tear gas, water cannons, and razor wire fences along its borders with Serbia and Croatia, demanding that migrants line up at designated openings. Hungarians—my own family members—were labeled racist and xenophobic. This hurt and angered me profoundly.

Having lived through Nazism and communism, Hungarians more than understand the desire to flee oppression and conflict. My father and mother both fled from communism; my stepfather, her partner of forty years, escaped the 1956 Soviet invasion of Hungary by crossing the border with Austria on foot: he and a group of friends from the village school climbed barbed-wire fences and dodged sentries in watchtowers. Two of them died in the attempt. Britain allowed my parents and stepfather in as part of a democratically determined asylum policy, and I will forever be grateful for that. But let's be clear: the British government made that decision, not the EU, since at that time the EU didn't exist in its present form and Britain wasn't a member anyway.

In 2015, Hungarians may or may not have been against granting refugees sanctuary, but is it fair that they never had the chance to decide the right policy for themselves in the first place? When power remains close to the people, they are confident in their ability to control their own fate, and the best side of human nature comes to the fore. People create space for others. But when power is centralized in the hands of the elite, whether that's grandstanding politicians or unelected bureaucrats, people turn on each other, panicked that they have lost control over their own destiny. How grotesquely offensive for the powerful elites to look down their noses at anxious, powerless citizens and deliberately smear their reasonable concerns as closed-minded bigotry.

Americans who live in states that share a border with Mexico can probably sympathize with Hungarians quite easily. For years, they have had to contend with the coastal elites scolding them that immigration is good for the economy and good for "diversity" so they should stop complaining about the steady stream of people unlawfully entering a country founded on the rule of law. What the elites don't see is how uncontrolled immigration changes the rest of their country. "Regions and cities with the largest immigrant populations are often the wealthiest and most dynamic," writes *New York Times* columnist Ross Douthat. But "the hinterlands are also filled with people who might want to move to wealthier regions (or who used to live there) but can't because an immigrants-and-professionals ecosystem effectively prices out the middle class." The elitists see either people like them or new immigrants, both succeeding on their own terms, but fail to see the millions left behind elsewhere. They are unresponsive to the concerns of those millions because they barely know that they or their problems exist. As a result, the social fabric frays. Communities become anxious, trust breaks down, and perfectly reasonable concerns get smeared as racism and xenophobia, ensuring that trust breaks down still further.

Let me be perfectly clear: I am pro-immigration; I consider myself an immigrant two times over. But that's exactly why I believe in sovereign nation-states controlling their borders properly:

I know the difference that a country can make. A whole host of factors—history, culture, economy, geography—go into determining the nation part of a nation-state, and nations are not infinitely elastic, even one as diverse and as accepting as the United States. This point was made powerfully by President Barack Obama in his 2006 autobiography, *The Audacity of Hope*. Not all the fears of working-class voters (white and black) "are irrational," then Senator Obama wrote. While acknowledging the many benefits of immigration, Obama conceded the valid concerns of many: "Native-born Americans suspect that it is they, and not the immigrant, who are being forced to adapt." And he expressed a common irritation of many Americans. "If I'm honest with myself, I must admit that I'm not entirely immune to such nativist sentiments," Obama wrote. "When I see Mexican flags waved at pro-immigration demonstrations, I sometimes feel a flush of patriotic resentment. When I'm forced to use a translator to communicate with the guy fixing my car, I feel a certain frustration."

As these passages testify, immigration is not just an economic issue. In Chapter 2 we considered the impact of immigration on jobs and wages; here in our discussion of the Populist Society we have to acknowledge the impact of immigration on social cohesion, too. That's partly about who comes here, and partly about how they are treated once they have arrived.

The truth is that consent for immigration depends on control of immigration. If American citizens are confident that the people they elect are in control of deciding who comes to live and work here, they will be welcoming and neighborly. But if they suspect or know that either through sheer incompetence, or worse, through the imposition of an open-borders ideology that has never been put on the ballot anywhere in America, the ruling elite is not in control of who comes here—if in fact pretty much anyone who wants to can come to America—then consent for immigration will collapse. And that's a disaster for our social fabric. It undermines trust between the people and their government, and among the people themselves.

A nation's immigration policy should treat every immigrant and would-be immigrant fairly and justly, and refugees should be given sanctuary as much as is practically possible. But all countries, including the United States, have their limits. The elite's open-borders ideology fails to recognize this. It was born in an age before the Internet and instant communication stoked the demand for mass global migration, and before cheap international travel helped provide the supply. Both the demand and the supply are of course incentivized to grow if there is widespread awareness of lax immigration control. Conversely, tight immigration control helps reduce migration flows, thereby reducing the human and financial cost of dealing with large numbers of illegal immigrants. In fact, the optimal number of illegal immigrants is zero, and that should be the goal set by any government.

The job doesn't stop there, however. Once immigrants are here, we need to make sure they are treated right. It should of course go without saying that racism and xenophobia should never be tolerated. But when we think of immigration in the context of social cohesion, there's another important factor, too: integration. One of the biggest policy disasters in the United Kingdom in recent years was the elitists' embrace of "multiculturalism," the idea that those from other cultures who came to Britain should be free to live according to the culture of the place they came from rather than being expected to adapt to British culture. This explains, in part, the phenomenon that prompted the British government to commission its own report on social cohesion, which produced alarming evidence of segregated communities, including Muslim-dominated communities where women are denied their basic rights on a widespread basis. One of the factors enabling the subjugation of Muslim women was the refusal of the men who controlled their households to allow women to learn English. Both in general and specific terms, this provides an important warning to America.

British policy makers wrestling with the evident failures of the multiculturalist approach would often point to America as a positive counterexample: a society where immigrants cherish and proudly display their roots, but nevertheless embrace a shared identity as Americans, with everything that goes with that—values, social norms, language. That positive expression of national identity is one of the great strengths of America, but increasingly it seems as if it is being undermined from within. That's a trend we have to resist: we must not allow the growth of segregated communities where English is not spoken and where values and behavior that undermine the rights laid out in the Constitution are challenged or flouted.

Immigration is a sensitive subject and must be handled as such. We should always want to welcome people to America who want to make a positive contribution to our economy and our society; but that process must be tightly controlled with no exceptions. And once here we must insist that immigrants integrate with the country they have joined, not imitate the country they came from. That means speaking our language, accepting our values, and abiding by our Constitution.

That is only reasonable. That is Positive Populism.

2. TRADE AND CHINA

Open borders' equally misguided ideological sidekick is "free trade." Both make the rich richer and help people in other countries improve their living conditions. Since the 1990s, this neatly packaged win-win narrative has dominated political discourse among both Republicans and Democrats alike—if there's one thing the foreign policy establishments of both parties agree on, it's free trade pacts and more immigration. But these twin policies have been far from a win-win for the working Americans who have fallen behind.

Of course, trade is a good thing. It helps create jobs and opportunity, it gives entrepreneurs the chance to expand their horizons; it gives consumers more choices and lower prices. Hooray. The question is, what are the terms on which companies trade with their counterparts in other countries? In practice, there is very little free trade. There are endless international agreements governing trade, many of them involving relatively obscure issues like aligning regulatory standards and establishing dispute mechanisms. The political argument over trade—the place where the populist agenda most directly challenges the elitist consensus of the past few decades—is over the distribution of the economic benefits of today's international trading system. And there are two key elements in that discussion: tariffs and China.

Tariffs are basically a tax on imports. Throughout modern history, countries have imposed tariffs on imported goods in order to raise money and to protect domestic producers from cheap competition. (Countries also use what are known as "non-tariff barriers" to control trade, for example placing limits on certain import categories.) All countries have tariffs and quotas, including the United States and the European Union. Not even the United States and Canada, which have among the world's closest trading relationships (shared over the longest unprotected border in the world), have completely free trade. But since the end of World War II, there has been a clear international consensus that economies benefit the most when barriers to trade are as low as possible. In part, the postwar move to lower tariffs and other barriers aimed to help defeated and impoverished countries like Germany, Japan, and China recover and prosper, creating opportunity for stronger economies like America's to sell more exports to them.

Based on this thinking, America adopted an extremely open posture on international trade, lowering tariffs on imports to America even if other countries maintained tariffs and other barriers on American exports. The United States was so clearly the world's leading economy that this imbalance didn't matter. America powered ahead in the decades after the end of the war, and the trend toward more free trade—lower tariffs and trade barriers—accelerated in the late 1980s and '90s with the new era of globalization, where a combination of better communications and financial deregulation turbo-charged international commerce. US business leaders transformed their outlook from an American to a global one. Financial markets rewarded profitability and shareholder returns, and executives were incentivized accordingly. If a product could be made for a fraction of the cost in another country and then shipped back to America for a lower price than would be possible to achieve back home, well, that's what would be done.

The effect on American workers or their communities didn't factor in. Why would it? It doesn't show up on a spreadsheet—except as a cost reduction. So the big business elite lobbied politicians to make it easier for them to go global—to operate wherever they could and to ship products across international borders in any way that would deliver a better return for shareholders and of course higher pay for themselves.

This is how the leaders of the political establishment, in both main parties, turned themselves into the stooges of corporate America.

But now we see the reckoning. There's no question that this globalization of the economy helped poor people in poor countries get richer as international investment flooded into places like

Mexico, China, and Vietnam. There's no question that rich people in rich countries got richer as the business elite reaped the rewards of higher profitability and growth. And there's no question that consumers in America and other wealthy nations also benefited, in the form of cheaper products imported from overseas. But the impact on working people in rich countries, especially those employed in industries most vulnerable to cheaper imports, like manufacturing, was devastating. As we saw in Chapter 1, the resulting job losses and income stagnation (or decline) caused searing pain for decades in many parts of America.

The globalist response is to say, well, that's the result of market forces. Of course no one wants to see jobs lost and wages go down. But it's a competitive world, and if you put barriers in the way, the American people will just get hurt differently, for example through higher prices as a result of higher tariffs on imports.

The positive populist, on the other hand, would say: Sure, we believe in market forces, too. But let's focus on our domestic market at home, and the impact of any particular trade arrangement on domestic industries and workers. If lowering a given barrier puts American industries at an unfair disadvantage or would threaten the livelihoods of a substantial number of American workers, why should we consent to that? How can we expect our companies and workers to compete with foreign subsidies or lax regulations? Shouldn't there be a level playing field? Shouldn't we match other countries' tariffs? And if that means higher costs for imported goods, why can't you big businesses absorb that for once, and pay your executives and shareholders a bit less? Why is it always working people whose jobs are sent overseas, who seem to bear the brunt of any negative change?

This debate over trade gets to the heart of the elitist class structure. Members of the elite have a global outlook because that's how they are rewarded. The CEO of an American company with global operations is moving pieces around a global chessboard. He or she is not incentivized to favor American workers over any other workers. The incentives are to find the cheapest workers.

In no instance has this globalist outlook been more faithfully implemented than with America's ever-expanding trade relationship with China. For a long time, our economic interaction with China was minimal. That all changed when, with US backing, China joined the World Trade Organization in 2000. The elites argued that by integrating China into the world economy, we would benefit financially through increased, mutually beneficial trade and investment, and that we would benefit strategically by moving China away from communism toward openness and maybe even democracy. Of course the exact opposite happened, on both fronts. Over the next few years, manufacturing jobs in America were destroyed on a massive scale as China used its newfound access to "dump" its state-subsidized exports into the American and world markets. And instead of moving toward democracy, China has become ever more authoritarian and aggressive. The only difference is that now, it is incomparably richer and more empowered to assert its hegemonic mania—thanks to the elite's catastrophic misjudgment.

Both Presidents George W. Bush and Barack Obama pathetically failed to stand up to China's economic imperialism and global expansionism. Neither had the backs of working Americans; instead they just wanted to look like good global players to their Big Business donors and foreign policy experts—all of whom are now utterly humiliated as the true scale of the establishment's China debacle becomes apparent. The greedy, foolish elites were mesmerized by the prospect of untold riches from China's untapped consumer markets—little realizing that China would never be as stupid as we were, and allow foreign competitors to get the edge.

The gullible and naive "Asia experts" labored under the impression that if we gave China the Olympics, if we engaged on China's terms, if we got China into the trading system, then China would become more democratic, human rights would improve, and we would all be a lot richer.

Well, the Chinese got richer. And the elites in America got richer. But is China any more democratic? No; it has regressed, if that is possible, from communist oligarchy to an increasingly totalitarian state. Is China playing by the rules? No; it is quite literally taking islands from its neighbors, ignoring international rulings, and flouting agreed maritime boundaries. Instead of playing by the established rules of the international community it is actively setting its own, creating a network of quiescent countries—including in Europe—through its "One Belt, One Road" infrastructure initiative. Its aggressive cyberwarfare against America has included not only industrial espionage but the theft of Americans' personal data on a massive scale. Meanwhile, Chinese industry continues to undercut American manufacturing, totally disproportionate tariffs are levied on foreign imports to China, and currency manipulation further puts our exporters at an unfair disadvantage. Even when China does allow American corporations to compete in its markets, it's entirely on the regime's terms: American companies cannot own their own Chinese businesses, they can only operate through joint ventures. And for technology companies, a condition of operation is to hand over commercial secrets in vital areas like artificial intelligence (AI) and quantum computing. The Chinese have turned intellectual property theft into a weapon of war.

I hate to say I told you so—but I told you so.

Against the grain of the elitists' embarrassing China swoon, I argued all along that no good would come of this. In Downing Street I typically stayed away from foreign policy but I did have one early victory as I persuaded David Cameron, in the teeth of frantic protests from the British Foreign Office and Treasury, that his first major international visit as prime minister should be to India, not China. Of course, the corrupt apparatchiks of Beijing, by now accustomed to more than a decade of craven kowtowing by the supine West, were infuriated. And sure enough, the China-skeptic posture I advocated was reversed as soon as I left, culminating in the abject humiliation of a lavish state visit to Britain for the brutal dictator Xi Jinping, paraded through the streets of London in a golden carriage while goons from the Chinese embassy beat up pro-democracy protesters just a few feet away.

Well, now we know. We can't pretend that China wants anything less than world domination—economically, technologically, politically, militarily. We can't waste time hoping it will play by our rules. It won't. Some say China just wants to set its own rules. But China doesn't want to play by *any* rules. The sooner we realize that, the sooner we can take the aggressive stance we need to isolate this rising giant of a rival. We once put all our might into fighting and winning the Cold War against the Soviets; the Chinese regime is an infinitely bigger threat because unlike the Soviet Union it is an economic powerhouse. Military conflict between China and America isn't inevitable, and I'm not advocating that we go down that path. But for our long-term prosperity, and for a world run according to the values of openness and democracy, we must take aggressive action now, even at the cost of short-term pain.

To start, we have to get tough on our trade imbalances with China. Imposing tariffs on more imports and blocking access to our markets in other ways may well raise prices for Americans—but it is the only way to make the Chinese reconsider the status quo they have enjoyed for the past thirty years, since they began their quest to enter the World Trade Organization. China was admitted in 2001, but with the status of a "non-market economy" that allows its trading partners wider discretion to levy tariffs on their state-subsidized imports. Now China wants its status updated to "market economy," which would inhibit its trading partners' options. China has learned how to rig the WTO's rules for its own gain in this multilateral arena, and working Americans are the ones suffering.

But we can and should go further than that. When I was at Oxford, I proudly joined protests against apartheid South Africa. Its regime was rightly an international pariah for its despicable treatment of the majority of its people. I don't understand why China isn't any less of a pariah today than South Africa was then. A brutal dictatorship, China oppresses its people, is building an Orwellian social surveillance system, bullies its neighbors, and flouts the established norms of global trade and politics. We need to move quickly to counter its aggressive behavior and seize the initiative.

It's time for a complete economic boycott of China. We can start by imposing exactly the same conditions on Chinese companies in America as the ones imposed on American companies in China: no independent operations, compulsory joint ventures, and the forced handover of intellectual property. How long do you think Chinese companies would stay here on that basis? Next: no American company or investor should be permitted to support China's various schemes for world domination, like "One Belt, One Road" and "Made In China 2025." All US companies in China should pull out, and no new investments should be made. Yes, this seems drastic, but in the long run it is our only hope of putting sufficient pressure on the vile Beijing regime that it might collapse from within. We won the Cold War by accepting the high price and being determined to pay it, in the form of a defense buildup that the Soviets could not match. China is in an infinitely stronger position than the Soviet Union was then, so the price will be so much higher.

But we have to be prepared to pay it. China is our enemy, not our "partner," and we need to start acting like it.

3. MAXIMIZE SOVEREIGNTY—NOT MULTILATERALISM

Every January, the world's self-appointed ruling elite descends on a small ski resort in the Swiss Alps named Davos. In a bacchanal to excess, CEOs, hedge fund tycoons, central bankers, and rock stars, ferried by more than one thousand private jets, come together for a champagne-sipping, fondue-sharing week of smug self-congratulation on finding themselves literally on top of the world. I had the misfortune of attending the World Economic Forum, as it's officially called, with David Cameron. I couldn't wait to leave and promised myself never to attend again.

One reason I despise the summitry of the global elitists is that no matter how much they profess their fidelity to values like democracy and human rights, it is power and money that really talk. Sure, there are some pariahs like North Korea and Syria's Bashar al-Assad, but even the world's worst autocrats—like Russia's Vladimir Putin or Turkey's Recep Erdogan—and most obscene oligarchs are welcomed at Davos with open arms. The World Economic Forum isn't a multinational organization per se. But it mimics the balefully amoral behavior of so many international institutions—the WTO (which allows China to get away with currency manipulation and dumping), the UN (which appointed former Zimbabwean dictator Robert Mugabe a "goodwill ambassador," put the genocidal Syrian regime on a committee to fight the "exploitation of people," and punished a whistle-blower for trying to protect Chinese dissidents), the World Bank and International Monetary Fund, or IMF (both of which have used so-called development aid to extract predatory loans on sovereign countries and then use them to force massively disruptive economic changes that benefit wealthy foreign investors)—to name a few. What they all have in common is that the bureaucrats are in charge, bureaucrats who are so besotted with their own privileges that they let corrupt autocrats, rapacious kleptocrats, avaricious bankers, and cynical CEOs get away with anything so long as they say the right thing on the right platform at the right summit.

Of course, positive populists are not isolationists; we understand we can benefit from globalization. But globalism is not the same as globalization. We reject the self-serving ideology of open borders, open capital, and unelected technocracy perpetuated by the elites for the elites. The globalist manifesto argues that our nation's affairs should be governed by multilateral institutions—that the edicts of bodies like the WTO, EU, IMF, and World Bank should have primacy over national bodies like democratically elected governments. And therein lies globalism's fatal flaw: it is not democratic. Even if we concede the wisdom of global bureaucrats, it is clear that they are not accountable to people. They have their own agenda and by centralizing decision making, they give themselves the power to implement that agenda free of any democratic checks or balances. On those grounds alone globalism is unacceptable, even when it delivers positive outcomes.

An argument against globalism isn't an argument against internationalism. Nation-states have long benefited from exchange of people, goods, and ideas with other countries. But something that for centuries was a natural and organic expression of human curiosity and ingenuity has more recently become fetishized as an absolute and mechanistic end in itself, as elitists have subjugated the notion of nationhood to globalism, something they see as more righteous and noble.

But it's neither righteous nor noble to place the interests of the corporate bottom line (driven, of course, by personal financial incentives to do so) ahead of the interests of working people in your own country—your neighbors. Globalism's tangible impact is seen in the decision to relocate the factory, to "offshore" the call center, to discontinue the product and brand in favor of one that can be sold in the same way everywhere on earth. Because that's more "efficient."

The positive populist doesn't begrudge international cooperation—even multilateral cooperation. But if the system is ever to be accountable, it needs to be dismantled and replaced with case-by-case alliances between sovereign states. There's nothing unreasonable about the idea that America needs to look out for its own interests; Germany needs to look out for its; Mexico, its; and so on down the list. Nation-states should cooperate when they determine that it's the right thing to do, not because some bureaucracy requires it.

Writing in the *Wall Street Journal* in 2017 ("Five Eyes Are Better Than One"), Walter Russell Mead demonstrates how simply and effectively sovereign nations can work together on an ad hoc basis, rather than in formalized, impotent, consensus-seeking bureaucracies. The "five eyes" are an expression used by the Anglophone intelligence community to refer to the United States, Canada, the United Kingdom, Australia, and New Zealand. It's a completely unofficial, nonbureaucratic relationship in which these countries exchange information with one another through secure channels, like good neighbors do. Writes Mead:

> There is no formal requirement that they act together. They have no joint decision-making process. Teams of diplomats

don't negotiate long and detailed memorandums governing their plans for common action. Nor do these countries force a consensus where one doesn't exist. Each partner moves at its own speed, on its own path, and there is no obligation or expectation that they will agree with one another or work together on every issue. Each of the Five Eyes countries is jealous of its independence. They seek to maximize their sovereignty through cooperation rather than pooling it.

The Five Eyes—free of a preening director-general or bloated secretariat—accomplishes its mission perfectly.

Countries can and should work together to make important strategic and policy decisions. But instead of doing it at absurd summits run by bureaucrats, ministers and leaders should meet according to their rules, not someone else's. When two countries have a dispute between them, *they* should determine how it is mediated, and no one else. The globalist bureaucracies created in the wake of World War II served a purpose once, accustoming a whole generation of leaders to formalized relationships on defense, trade, and foreign policy. But like training wheels on a bike, we no longer need the heavy hand of these organizations to guide us. We know our interests, and understand our relationships. Where alliances have served us well, like NATO, we'll push forward. But there's no need to perpetuate bureaucracies that have acquired their own agendas and their own leaders who swan around as if they themselves are the ones chosen by the voters.

Good fences make good neighbors: jealously independent, maximizing sovereignty, cooperating with other sovereign nation-states in a world that's growing more interconnected and less violent. . . . That's the way to help rebuild allegiance to a shared national story, a vital part of the Populist Society.

IN A NUTSHELL ...

Americans should embrace the nation-state as an integral part of our social fabric. But patriotism does not equal nationalism, and Positive Populism channels patriotism toward strengthening our own nation, not tearing down others.

1. Immigration and social cohesion: Americans should never doubt that theirs is a land of immigrants and opportunity, but consent for immigration depends on control of immigration, and uncontrolled immigration—especially when immigrants eschew integration—destroys the social fabric.

2. Trade and China: Trade works only when it is fair and it benefits American workers; trade with China has been one-sided. The cruel, corrupt, authoritarian dictatorship in Beijing is our enemy, not our partner, and it must be confronted and defeated. We need to implement a total economic boycott of China.

3. Maximize sovereignty—not multilateralism: Countries must engage on the world stage as equal, sovereign partners, not the pawns of undemocratic, unaccountable international institutions.

THE
POPULIST
GOVERNMENT

I N ONE FORM OR ANOTHER, YOU'VE HEARD THE TERM *people power* a lot in this book. That's because it is central to the idea of populism. In areas like school choice or local civic engagement, we've already seen how Positive Populism can put power in people's hands. But to really see its full, empowering potential, we need a program for actual, concrete reform of our democracy. We need to define and work toward the Populist Government.

The mistake made by many of the politicians who talk about "fixing government" is to pick one problem over another, thereby asking incomplete questions: Too big or too small? Too much spending or too little? Too streamlined or too weak? Yes, these things are important, but to enact the populist agenda, we need to do much more than reduce the size and scope of government and decentralize power (though we should).

Instead, we need a new set of questions, questions that will guide us as we rethink government altogether. It's not enough just to slash spending, cut taxes, or repeal unnecessary rules. We need to determine which problems ought to be decided in Washington, the states, or in our neighborhoods. And whom do we trust to make decisions? Do we delegate power, or exercise it ourselves?

Above all, the Populist Government is about accountability. Elitists have grown accustomed to a system in which no matter who's in power, they're still in charge. Insulated from the consequences of their decisions, the actual results of a given program matter little to them. So long as they are reelected—or get that big lobbying gig.

We need to take power back from the elitists—in Washington, the statehouse, and in city hall. A country as large and complex as the United States can never be a purely direct democracy—and that was never the aim of the Founders. In Franklin's famous phrase, it is "a Republic, if you can keep it." But time and time again, Americans have shown that when trusted with power, they exercise it prudently. How can we infuse that spirit of civic-mindedness in our politics? And how can government reflect the most dynamic elements of our society, and not the most staid and moribund?

The populist agenda can be enacted only by truly Populist Government. The point of Positive Populism is to show how we get there—to a government that serves the people fairly and judiciously.

7

LOCAL

"ALL POLITICS IS LOCAL," they say. Well, not enough to-day.

That's why the positive populist is, at heart, a devolutionist. We want to keep power in the hands of the people, to decentralize it whenever possible. Going in the other direction, ceding power to a higher and inevitably more distant authority, should only happen when necessary—after a high burden of proof has been demonstrated. That's what a populist means by "limited government." Local, close to the people. That's the kind of government we need.

That's the kind of government colonial Americans thought we needed, too. The American Revolution is rightly celebrated for establishing the first true republic in the modern world, but in many ways the Revolution was the culmination of one that had started well before. From the outset, the British colonies in North America were run locally. "Salutary neglect," it was called; London stayed far away from colonial affairs, handling trade, defense, and not much else. Each colony was allowed to develop its own characteristic government, suited to its needs. We might chafe now to recall the decidedly *un*democratic hereditary governments in Pennsylvania and Maryland or Massachusetts' Puritan theocracy. But while some of those experiments were odious, especially those based on slavery, others helped America establish many of its emblematic traits, including religious liberty and personal freedom.

It was infringement of those liberties and the perception that the implicit "deal" of self-government was being violated that led Americans to rebel from the British crown in 1775. But the subsequent revolution merely confirmed America's independent streak. Even today, the images of town militias, Sons and Daughters of Liberty, and other grassroots groups loom large. The government that resulted from the American Revolution reflected Americans' experience with British misrule. Americans distrusted the government in London for all sorts of reasons, but chief among them was its centralization. How could a small coterie of officials rule a continent they had never visited, three thousand miles away? It would be a ridiculous concept to justify now, in the age of the Internet and mobile phones, let alone in the age of the sail, when it took six weeks for a letter to cross the Atlantic.

That suspicion of central authority rightly stayed with Americans as they formed their new government, which was codified with the Constitution and the Bill of Rights. Those documents explicitly created a weak executive, a powerful legislature, and a decentralization of power, with sovereignty afforded to the states. Americans continued that tradition in their local government, especially as they expanded westward. Without established elites or gentry, Americans found themselves creating towns from scratch. Far from the population centers of the east, they had to rely on one another for their mutual welfare. Early Americans weren't subjects but full participants in their communities. Democracy wasn't given to them; they created it. "The health of a democratic society," French writer Alexis de Tocqueville declared in his iconic *Democracy in America*, upon witnessing American governance in action, "may be measured by the quality of functions performed by private citizens."

Of course, quoting Tocqueville on American democracy is hardly original. But the reason his work was so noteworthy is that he knew he was witnessing a singular event in human history. American democracy was not rooted in the new nation's capital. The more local, the better: states rather than Congress; towns rather than states. But as America developed, cities grew, suburbs sprang up, and we lost that early ethos. Local government was subsumed by state government, and then federal government. Despite the better impulse of those pioneering Americans two centuries ago, the result today is that democracy has drifted away from the people it serves, becoming less and less accountable.

"You don't know what you've got till it's gone," goes the famous song lyric. In Britain, we never had "it"—truly local government—in the first place. When we entered Downing Street in 2010 as the new administration, the average size of population for the lowest tier of executive government was an astounding 151,110. And the results were stark: the councilors elected in such a system could not possibly know their constituents, and their constituents could not know them. These local elected officials were well-intentioned volunteers, but with names barely recognizable and little reputational stake in a municipality's improvement. Voters had no idea who was running their towns and cities. Worse, with successive waves of centralization from previous governments (both Labour and Conservative), bureaucratic control was replacing democratic accountability. The will of local communities was routinely second-guessed by London bureaucrats micromanaging the activities of local councils.

It seemed so different in America, with strong, visible, dynamic mayors like New York's Rudy Giuliani and Mike Bloomberg, renowned even in the United Kingdom for their creative—sometimes risky—policies to revitalize and polish the Big Apple. It was different, too, just across the English Channel in France, where mayors were the most admired part of the political system—from the thousands of small-town mayors serving an average of less than two thousand residents, to the big-city mayoral positions that were often a stepping-stone to the presidency of the republic.

But in the British system of local government, there were no mayors. I was determined that we should introduce them, convinced that the clear accountability that comes from a single elected municipal leader would transform the effectiveness of local government. And so it became part of the Conservative Party's election platform, with David Cameron proudly promising that he "want[ed] to be the first prime minister that leaves office having given away power, rather than accumulating it." How demoralizing, then, that soon after taking office, our plans for introducing powerful elected mayors in Britain's major cities were sabotaged by our own government ministers, too timid to challenge the lobbying efforts of the anonymous local councilors who feared losing their power to a strong, directly elected local leader. I tell this story because it viscerally demonstrates how hard it is to deliver promises of devolution. Citizens thirst for control over their own affairs; when offered a chance at self-rule, people seize it. But the elites resist it.

America doesn't need more mayors because it already has thousands of them. But that doesn't mean American government is sufficiently local: far from it. Where America falls down is not devolution, per se, but duplication. With agencies making rules and carrying out policy at the federal, state, and local levels—not to mention various special districts—it's nearly impossible to know who's responsible for what. That makes it harder for well-meaning public servants to do their jobs (imagine trying to enforce a rule only to be told you're infringing on another agency's jurisdiction). But most of all, overlapping jurisdictions make accountability all but impossible. Who runs the schools? Whose responsibility is it to clean up after a hurricane? Who determines whether a marriage license can be granted or denied to a same-sex couple? If the government barely knows who's responsible for what, how can citizens know whom to turn to? Or hold accountable? Take one expert account:

> There are 12 different agencies that deal with exports. There are at least five different agencies that deal with housing policy. Then there's my favorite example: the Interior Department is in charge of salmon while they're in freshwater, but the Commerce Department handles them when they're in saltwater. I hear it gets even more complicated once they're smoked.

Those aren't the words of some small-government conservative. They're from a speech given by Barack Obama as president. Even he recognized that the system is a mess. It's a gift to the lobbyists and special interests. The more complicated government is, the easier it is for insiders to manipulate the process. And the more centralized it is, the easier it is for malicious actors—whether that's hostile foreign powers or random hackers—to mount crippling attacks. Centralized government is not just more unaccountable; it's more fragile. So let's make it simpler by returning power to the people and taking a clear-eyed look at what functions should be carried out at which level. The aim should be to push power down—all the way. From the federal government to the states, from the states to local government, and then even beyond that: from local government to the neighborhood. That should be the next revolution for American democracy.

1. FROM THE FEDS TO THE STATES

The centralization we see today in America is not what it was supposed to be like. From the beginning, power was enshrined with the states, not the central government. States have their own constitutions, after all, because in many ways they are sovereign. Even the name—United States of America—speaks to the notion of a federation more than a monolithic country. That sentiment was codified in the Tenth Amendment to the US Constitution: "The powers not delegated to the United States by the Constitution, nor prohibited by it to the States, are reserved to the States respectively, or to the people."

How empty that promise looks today. Despite the Tenth Amendment, the federal government reaches down from Washington, DC, interfering in all sorts of areas "not delegated to the United States" and imposing costly regulations and unfunded mandates on individual states. These power grabs by the federal government have been aided and abetted by the federal judiciary, which has sided with the executive and legislative branches' desire to acquire more power. The centralizing impulse has been a consistent and bipartisan trend: both Republicans and Democrats, conservatives and liberals, are guilty of hoarding power.

One of the reasons that power has slipped away from the states, despite the clear intent of the Constitution, is that when power is seized by the center, it is often motivated by a well-intentioned desire to ensure equitable outcomes that might not otherwise be achieved. The most glaring example of states' rights necessitating a constitutional pruning remains slavery. America's worst blemishes are associated with white supremacists who cloak themselves in "states' rights" rhetoric. And a desire to make the federal government smaller is not arguing against government out of hand. Government performs vital functions, including at the national level, and especially when it comes to something as fundamental as civil rights. If the states are literally violating the spirit and the letter of the Constitution, federal interference is more than called for. But does anyone really believe that the federal government today limits itself to such cases? Of course not. Nevertheless, politicians and bureaucrats in Washington have convinced themselves of their indispensability to good government throughout every nook and cranny of America. Thus they have, contrary to both the letter and the spirit of the Constitution, asserted their power in a range of areas—from healthcare to welfare to business and environmental regulation to education—that they have no business getting involved with. Remind you of anything?

"The history of the Federal Government is a history of repeated injuries and usurpations, all having in direct object the establishment of an absolute Tyranny over these States."

Yes, it's the Declaration of Independence again. Just as in the Introduction, changing the words leads to a pretty accurate picture of the relationship between the European Union and its member states, in modern America, if you change "King of Great Britain" to "Federal Government," the rest of that pithy phrase pretty much describes the present reality. Fortunately, the founding document that followed a decade or so after the Declaration provides a practical remedy for the "injuries and usurpations" of federal centralization. Despite what the lawyers might have you believe, the US Constitution is populist in spirit: it built in mechanisms to challenge power-hungry elitists in the capital. Article V gives states the ability to amend the Constitution as necessary through a constitutional convention. Those amendments to the Constitution can be proposed without congressional initiative: Congress would simply need to vote on the amendments proposed, knowing the whole country is watching, keeping them accountable.

We need a revolutionary transfer of power from the federal government to the states, and the only way we're going to get it is to do what the Framers allowed us to. One energetic group wants to do exactly that, to hold what they call a Convention of the States, which would advance amendments designed to limit the powers of the federal government and undo much of the centralization that has shifted power to Washington, DC. Possible amendments include term limits on Congress and the federal judiciary, a balanced-budget amendment, and requirements for new legislation to have sunset clauses, so that future generations might have a chance to renew or reject a given policy.

You don't have to agree with every proposed amendment offered by the convention's supporters to agree that the best way to give power back to the people is through a dramatic (but peaceful) shock. Let's face it: the ruling elite in Washington will never surrender power. Democrats won't do it; Republicans won't do it; none of them will do it, however much they say they believe in it, because in the end there is nothing that politicians and bureaucrats want more than power. So we're going to have to take it from them against their will, and a constitutional convention is the best chance we have.

But we shouldn't stop there; we should keep going, pushing power lower and closer to the people.

2. FROM STATES TO CITIES

While states are sovereign, with their own constitutions, municipalities are not. They live at the whim of state legislators and bureaucrats in often far-off state capitals. Frankly, those legislators enjoy that distance from the people affected by their decisions—it allows them to minimize scrutiny. It's no surprise that one Harvard study found a correlation between isolated state capitals and corruption. And even if not corrupt, the isolation certainly undermines accountability.

New York City's deteriorating transportation system is a case in point. The subways are run by the Metropolitan Transit Authority (MTA). You would think, since the entire subway system resides within the five boroughs, that the MTA would fall under the jurisdiction of the New York City transportation commissioner, who is appointed by the mayor. But that would be too easy. While the city does fund the MTA in part, it is in reality controlled by the governor in distant Albany, with veto power on essentially any major decisions over the system—a power that is consistently exercised. The New York State Legislature has added its stamp, rejecting a long list of measures designed to alleviate pressure on the system, even when those measures are overwhelmingly supported by New Yorkers desperate for a fix to their hellish commutes.

If cities truly had jurisdiction over their own affairs, we wouldn't just stop the unedifying spectacle of squabbling mayors and governors pointing fingers at one another, as the governor of New York and the mayor have done over the subway. Empowered to act, cities will take the initiative, and more often than not, they'll find solutions that work.

It needn't be just cities, though. In Chapter 2 we saw how a truly revolutionary reform of the school system would take power out of the hands of politicians and bureaucrats and put it in the hands of parents. But it's worth pointing out that a huge part of the problem right now is that education is controlled to an unbelievable degree at the state level. Rules on teacher recruitment and employment, curriculum and textbook choice, funding decisions—it's all determined by state legislators and superintendents around the country. They presume to know best for the children of their states, but how can they? How can anyone at the state level possibly conceive of the diverse needs of an individual school district or school?

Through my years in government, I found one thing over and over again: government elites consistently fail to understand the needs of the people they are trying to help. Either they are hopelessly removed from the problem, or, in cases of people in crisis, they have no feel for the background circumstances of those in need. That's why the closer we put government service delivery and policy making to the people it serves—from Washington to the states and states to the cities, the more effective, responsive, and democratic it will be.

3. TO THE NEIGHBORHOOD

Not everything can be totally decentralized. But more can be than you might think. In Chapter 5 I argued that for the most human of reasons (our inability to meaningfully relate to more than 150 or so people), the ideal unit of association and governance might actually be the neighborhood. We saw nongovernment applications of that principle: local volunteerism through "Civic Service," for example. But what about government itself? Could that be devolved to the neighborhood level? That was exactly the question I asked my team at 10 Downing Street years ago, and the answer I got was surprising.

It turned out that there was historical precedence for the kind of ultra-local devolution I was interested in exploring. In 1597, during Queen Elizabeth I's reign, Parliament passed a law ensuring that each district would have its own appointed overseers of the poor, who would determine how much money was needed to support the poor in that district and collect it from property owners; dispense food and money to the poor, as needed; and supervise the parish workhouse. Codified in 1601 along with earlier legislation aimed at helping the poor, this became known as the Elizabethan Poor Law Act. The overseers made sure orphans had apprenticeships so they learned a trade to support themselves later in life, and that the old and infirm were sheltered in almshouses. Distinctions were made at the local level between those who required "inside help" (institutionalization) or "outside help" (subsidies), and between the "deserving poor" (the sick and disabled) and the "undeserving poor" (the layabouts of the day). Though the Elizabethan era ushered in new compassion for the poor, begging was nonetheless prohibited (and harshly punished).

The language of the times offends the sensibilities of the modern ear, but I was struck by the Crown's attempt to push power down to the people at the parish level. There were fifteen thousand parishes in England and Wales at the time, which makes me think, in retrospect, that I didn't sound too far off when the *Spectator* magazine ran its 2015 headline, "We Need 10,000 Mayors—an Interview with Steve Hilton." But mayors and their defined city limits needn't be the lowest common denominator of governance. If the primary unit of government is city hall, the primary unit of society should be the neighborhood. New York City has eight and a half million residents—more than the entire state of Massachusetts, and roughly equivalent to Virginia. Houston is larger than fourteen states. Leaving every issue in the hands of its mayor is hardly people power at work.

The goal of decentralization shouldn't be a specific outcome. It should be a sense of greater participation and ultimately greater democracy and people power. Our guide should be to re-create the spirit of the Swiss "Landsgemeinden," the open-air assemblies dating back to 1294 that inspired French political philosopher Jean-Jacques Rousseau. In these assemblies, Rousseau wrote, the village men would gather outdoors to speak on any topic. Then the elders would count hands raised in favor or opposed, and the general will of the community would be discerned:

> When we see among the happiest people in the world bands of peasants regulating the affairs of state under an oak tree, and always acting wisely, can we help feeling a certain contempt for the refinements of other nations, which employ so much skill and effort to make themselves at once illustrious and wretched? . . . A state thus governed needs very few laws. . . .

Rousseau might have been overromanticizing the Swiss countryside and its peasantry. But in the Swiss, he saw a certain ideal of democracy come to life. That was also the spirit driving one of the most surprisingly effective policies enacted during the time I worked in government.

We know that it's no use simply exhorting people to "get involved" in their local communities: you need to give them a good reason for doing so. Something tangible. Well, there are few things more tangible at the neighborhood level than decisions about zoning. So we devised a way to take those decisions out of the hands of local councils (yes, even local councils can be distant from the people) and put them in the hands of the people directly affected by them: local residents. The idea was that any group of people, anywhere in the country, could come together and officially declare themselves a "Neighborhood." They would then follow an agreed consultative procedure in drawing up a "Neighborhood Plan." This plan would be unconstrained by any existing rules or regulations—whatever the neighborhood wanted could go in it. The plan would then have to be voted on in a local referendum, and if passed by a majority of residents would be binding—and overrule any zoning decision that a higher tier of government might wish to impose.

It was reminiscent of Rousseau, again:

> As long as several men assembled together consider themselves as a single body, they have only *one will* which is directed towards their common preservation and general well-being. . . . [T]he *common good* makes itself so manifestly evident that only common sense is needed to discern it.

Common sense instead of government rules. What an enlightened—and populist idea. Most observers at the time also considered it a crazy idea. When we explained how we wanted it to work, senior civil servants in the British government thought the whole thing was an elaborate joke. But the results justified our faith in the wisdom of people who have been given power to exercise: they tend to use it wisely. Thousands of Neighborhood Plans were developed and adopted, and in the vast majority of cases, rather than being a vehicle for NIMBYism, as critics feared, local neighborhoods chose to increase the amount of housing in their area. When government tries to impose things, people naturally resist. But when you trust them and give them power, they behave responsibly. That is Positive Populism in action.

In Portland, Oregon, neighborhoods were given official status with powers to propose policy ideas and have them considered and responded to: that led to the creation of neighborhood groups across the city fostering new community links and new ways for people to get together to effect change. Imagine how this kind of neighborhood liberation might work in more American towns and cities. Imagine Chicago's government allowing South Side residents to decide by popular vote where their neighborhood begins and ends. Once neighborhoods are better defined, there are many ways to give them more autonomy. Imagine how empowering it would be to decide what time the restaurants and bars close in your own neighborhood, regardless of what the rest of the city is doing. Or whether smoking and/or alcohol consumption should be permitted in your neighborhood's park. Perhaps a local road is too dangerous without a stop sign or a local factory is making too much noise at night. Imagine the flexibility available to you. Once people regain power over their communities, we should be confident that they will behave in ways that are responsible and mutually beneficial.

That can also be helped by localizing that vital but also sensitive role of government: policing. Policing is one of the most intimate relationships the community has with the state. Sir Robert Peel, founder of London's Metropolitan Police, the world's first modern police force, in the 1820s, placed community relations squarely at the center of his model: "The police are the public," he said, "and the public are the police."

But concerned with terrorism and organized crime, police in many major cities today have drifted away from that community-based model. For example, following the terrorist attacks of September 11, 2001, New York City's police department felt an understandable need to focus on national and international plots that could endanger residents. Members of the New York Police Department were stationed around the world, collecting potential intelligence on terrorism, and their training and equipment grew more militaristic. Fairly or not, a sense began to develop that the NYPD stood in opposition to residents, rather than with them.

When the NYPD's arrest of Staten Island resident Eric Garner in 2014 resulted in his death from a questionable chokehold technique, the force's leadership contemplated what it could do to improve its relations with the community. They decided to embrace Peel's community policing model by piloting a program called "neighborhood coordination officers," or NCOs. In the NCO program, a group of officers are assigned to a specific sector inside a precinct, where they will work every shift. They aren't transferred around a precinct, because the idea is to build a bond of trust inside a smaller sector, where they can get to know the residents on a first-name basis and understand the daily rhythms and cultures they are paid to serve and protect. Each of these sectors has two NCOs, officers who make their mobile phone numbers and personal email addresses available to residents. A large percentage of their time is devoted to meeting with residents of the sector, rather than responding to radio calls. Their precinct captains have been authorized to give NCOs the discretion to address percolating problems raised by residents in creative ways, before they escalate to criminal status. Like Queen Elizabeth's overseers of the poor before them, the NCOs are showing the way toward devolution that empowers people.

And here's one last, powerful way to put power directly into people's hands: literally give them the power of the purse. "Participatory budgeting" does just that. First implemented by a coalition of Brazilian Workers Party organizers and civil society activists in 1989 in an effort to bring the benefit of tax revenues down to those on the lower end of the economic scale, participatory budgeting encourages community members to involve themselves in the decision-making process over how to spend tax revenues. Of course, budgets and accounting can be mind-numbingly boring to many people. But as with so many things, it all depends on how you sell it. In Lisbon, Portugal, 10 percent of the city's budget has been set aside for participatory budgeting, with huge numbers getting involved and voting for projects as diverse as new parks and start-up hubs. Where it's been embraced, as it has in several American cities, participatory budgeting can be an effective tool for making sure the people's priorities are heard. The results are both tangible and tailored to the interests of the community—a positive populist example of the resultant good when government operates at the most local level possible.

For example, in Councilman Brad Lander's Brooklyn district, residents voted to fund $60,000 for a trailer with two showers for homeless people to use near a local soup kitchen; $300,000 to install air-conditioning in a very large and old elementary school; $200,000 for countdown clocks at bus stops near subways; and $70,000 to plant new trees along streets lacking them. Local officials in Boston, meanwhile, invited teens to vote on how to spend $1 million of city funds, and residents of Greensboro, North Carolina, voted to fund structures to provide shade over public pools and parking decks.

Encouraging community members to come forward and vote on a municipality's budget—or even a portion of that budget—is such a clear and tangible example of people power. Voting for candidates on election day, who may or may not enact their promises, or the priorities important to a community, can feel pointless—especially if the choice is between candidates representing the same elitist system. But coming together to directly determine the funding for a specific local need, and then actually seeing the results of your participation appear on the streets of your neighborhood, is not just a tangible way to make government more local. It's actually a way to restore people's faith in government itself, to convince them that in a democracy, they really can make a difference.

In and around our homes, government should be seen not just as a platform for putting people into office, but as a tool for improving our communities. It should always be as local as possible—and that is an awful lot more local than it is today. Giving people a stake in what happens on their streets so they're not always relying on some faraway entity to sort out their problems will restore the human quality to governance, tightening the natural bonds within communities and loosening the grip of distant elites.

IN A NUTSHELL . . .

We should reclaim the spirit in which the American Revolution was fought and the Tenth Amendment was written. Government should be as decentralized and as close to the people as possible—and that's a lot closer than it is today.

1. From the feds to States: Reverse the federal government's seemingly endless power grabs by calling a Convention of the States to uphold the decentralizing spirit of the Constitution.

2. From states to cities: Give cities the authority—and fiscal powers—they need to solve the problems they face.

3. To the neighborhood: Let neighborhoods govern themselves as much as is feasible, for example through neighborhood planning and participatory budgeting.

8

ENTREPRENEURIAL

A s WE'VE SEEN, there's no question that government in America has a lot of problems: it's too big, too centralized. But too often, we just leave it at that—especially those of us on the more conservative side of the political spectrum. All of us, even the most ardent small-government libertarian, would acknowledge that we need at least some government. The military is "government." So are the police. And the roads. However much we may hate it—and believe me, there are times when I have hated it more than most people alive—we can't do without government, and all the things that go with it: spending taxpayer money . . . bureaucracy . . . bureaucrats. It's unavoidable.

And the truth is, we don't spend enough time thinking positively about the kind of government that we do want to see. Yes, we should want it to be more local—so the ideas in Chapter 7 show how we might cut centralized and centralizing government down to size. But what should we do with what's left? What is the populist's positive vision for government?

I've thought about this a lot. It's a question I wrestled with in the highly centralized British government, and reflecting on that experience (some successes but mostly failures) has given me a clear-eyed view of what is needed. If we are truly to return power to the people, we cannot tinker. We need a rethink of government to make it more modern, more responsive, more effective. We need to make it, in a word, more entrepreneurial.

Republicans like to cite Ronald Reagan's powerful argument that government is not the solution to our problems, but the cause of them. (I actually prefer his more lighthearted quip: "The most terrifying words in the English language are 'I'm from the government and I'm here to help.'") He had a point. A good and big one. On a human level, many government workers are patriotic, hardworking Americans who genuinely want to do what's best. But bureaucrats are constrained by their surroundings. There is a centralizing impulse: a gravitational pull toward more spending, more programs, and more power. There is a bureaucratizing impulse: the instinctive reach for the red tape, the consultation, the endless evaluation. And perhaps most destructive of all there is the risk-averse impulse, an attitude of reflexive caution, resistance to new ideas, a bias toward inaction and "No."

People working in government simply don't work in a structure or culture that allows them or rewards them for doing things differently so they can achieve transformational results. Quite often, their goal is simply their agency's own perpetuation. And from a personal perspective, they know that the path to the top involves not rocking the boat. This is all such a waste. Government is the only institution that represents every citizen. As such, it has a moral responsibility to provide society's infrastructure: whether that's physical infrastructure—providing the roads, bridges, and utilities that a modern economy and society require, or human infrastructure—helping people find and maintain personal independence and flourish. This makes government essential for innovation. That might seem counterintuitive: after all, government often seems inimical to anything that could remotely be described as dynamic or new. But by laying the groundwork for people and businesses to grow, and setting the rules within which they operate, the state is essential in creating the room for entrepreneurs to invent and prosper. If only government could apply that same positive energy to itself.

1. INNOVATIVE GOVERNMENT

Think about some of the easiest things in your regular day-to-day life: Have food delivered. Order a ride from Uber or Lyft using your mobile device. Choose what to watch on Netflix or Hulu. Book a hotel room. Set your pet food order to a recurring cycle on Amazon.

These tasks require little thought and cause you minimal, if any, stress. Now think of some of the most complicated, aggravating things you do. File your taxes. Deal with the DMV. Apply for a zoning variation to build an extension on your home.

This second group of activities can drive you to despair, frustrated, stressed, enraged, and despondent with the government bureaucracies you encounter. That's because they've been designed for their own benefit, not yours; designed by bureaucrats, insensitive to people with limited time and bandwidth. As a result, services are poor and people suffer. Wouldn't it be better if public services prioritized the service part of their job?

How do we fix this? The answer, I learned shortly after arriving in California, is better design. When I came to Stanford University, I had the chance to teach a number of courses, including some at its Institute of Design, or "d.school." Teaching at Stanford required me to reflect on how we did things in government: what we did well, what we did badly, and what we could have done differently. Unsurprisingly, the run-ins with the bureaucracy loomed large in my mind. I started to realize why so many policies fail, why so much money is wasted, why so many promises are never delivered. It's not the ideologies of the leaders or the circumstances of the times, although obviously both are important. It's to do with the hopeless approach we take. An approach in which policy making is much more about theory than practice. Where the people making the policy, and the people implementing it, make no real effort to understand—in detail—the lives of the people who are on the receiving end.

I had no hesitation in saying to my students that the single biggest improvement we could bring to policy making in government would be to put people at the center of the process. That may sound platitudinous. But I mean it in a very precise way, based on the process of human-centered design—or, as it is known at the d.school, "design thinking."

At the d.school, students are guided through a process that, though inevitably messier in practice, can be explained in a handful of straightforward steps:

1. Empathize with the user

2. Define the problem

3. Generate ideas

4. Prototype solutions

5. Test the prototypes

. . . keep testing, adapting, and improving.

Let's start at the beginning of the process. *Empathize* is not a word you hear very much in government, but to understand a problem and imagine a solution requires that you understand the people whom it affects. This is an act of empathy, and human-centered designers put themselves in the shoes of those they are designing for. Empathy requires close, highly detailed observation of people, in the context in which they'll be using the product or service in question. This means talking to "users" before doing anything else, which really means listening to them. Politicians, of course, will say they listen to their constituents all the time, either directly or through polls and focus groups. But this is different. The kind of empathy work required for design thinking is about deeply understanding the life of the person you're designing for; forcing yourself to be open-minded rather than selling your own ideas.

So the first stage of the designers' process includes observing users in their day-to-day routines and immersing themselves in the user's environment for days, even weeks on end. Only then do you move to the second stage, defining the problem. This might seem straightforward, but it's surprising how frequently policy makers can be found solving the wrong problem—a superficial one, a symptom rather than a cause—or a problem perceived in one way by the outside world but totally differently by those actually experiencing it. For example, politicians who call for free community college tuition forget that for most college students, navigating the school bureaucracy and staying enrolled is more of a barrier than paying for it.

The next part of the design process is to come up with ideas—no shortage of them in government, but the truly revolutionary change would be for the public sector to adopt the final stages of design thinking: prototyping and testing an idea. The key is to embrace experimentation, testing a concept with cheap and rough prototypes before investing more in its development. This is a world away from how government does things. Yes, there are pilot programs—but these typically cost many millions of dollars and are launched with great fanfare. The incentive is to prove that they work. Prototype testing is not piloting. For example, rather than building a website for accessing government services (still a costly exercise), you could literally sketch it out on pieces of paper, put it in front of people, and get feedback on how they would use it based simply on asking them to point at boxes they would "click" on and why. The methodology of rapid and low-cost prototyping and testing that was developed and refined at Stanford's d.school is now the basic modus operandi for every tech firm in Silicon Valley, from the biggest names to the smallest start-ups.

So, how do we apply that ethos to government? Well, you could start by putting entrepreneurial people *into* government. Especially local government. That's exactly what Code for America does. It's like Teach For America or the Peace Corps—except for volunteers who want to help government bring services closer to the people. Code for America funds one-year fellowships for programmers, designers, and other technology workers, and embeds them in local governments (for example New York City's and Salt Lake County's) and federal agencies willing to accept their user-friendly design expertise. For example, Code for America fellows designed an app that uses text messaging to help parolees comply with their parole, and thus stay out of prison. Another gives families an easy way to find out what nutritional assistance they are eligible for and apply for it.

Code for America won't make American government more efficient overnight. But efforts like it, including various attempts to teach these design-thinking skills to civil servants and politicians directly, are starting to infuse the stifling culture of government with a sense of freshness and ingenuity. We should also aim to recruit more people adept at management to take executive roles in government. Business executives might not make the best politicians, but they do know how to manage teams, set priorities, and move cumbersome bureaucracies. Code for America's strapline is aspirational—some might say delusional: "What if all government services were this good?" But it's also subversive. It gets you thinking about what government could and should be, not what it shouldn't.

2. COMPETITIVE GOVERNMENT

When it comes to their software needs, tech entrepreneurs face a cost/benefit dilemma: Is it better to build what you need, or buy it ready-made from someone else? The answer differs in each case, but as a general rule, it only makes sense to build it yourself if you think you'll need to use it far into the foreseeable future, and you want to scale your business up.

This would be a useful way for government to think about its role. One of the reasons that government and the public sector can be so sclerotic is the assumption that government has to do everything itself. Literally run all the services directly, employing huge numbers of people. But beyond its ability (and responsibility) to set the rules, government's comparative advantage is not its ability to run things, or to bet on the future with other people's money. In some respects, government is the ultimate monopoly. Under the law, it has sole jurisdiction, and sole responsibility for the provision of services and public goods. But why should that mean it also has to deliver them? When the public sector is a monopoly provider, this creates an inherent dilemma for politicians and civil servants trying to make government more innovative. Innovation requires failure, or at least the possibility of it. But while a start-up can just pivot to a new product or a large corporation can do a write-off, a government monopoly that is delivering services to the public can't fail on a large scale without wasting taxpayer money—or worse, interrupt the provision of vital public services. They might even put lives at risk. Yes, prototyping and testing, as we saw above, is one way around this. But while that might help you experiment with new ideas, it won't result in systemic change across an existing government department.

So, while we should want government to be as innovative as possible, there is a limit as to how far we can push it as long as it is a monopoly provider.

One indirect way to promote innovation, an approach that avoids the dangers of top-down government reorganizations, which often cause disruption and cost for no discernible benefit, is to learn from one of the most important factors supporting entrepreneurialism in the private sector: competition.

For example, government can work with philanthropists, nonprofits, and private-sector companies to test risky new approaches to solving social problems. Initiatives like Bloomberg Philanthropies' Mayors Challenge, which gives $1–5 million prizes to cities that generate bold solutions to problems they face, are one way to go about it. But we can go much further. We saw in Chapter 3 the benefits that would flow from a much more aggressive stance on antitrust: breaking up established incumbents and breaking down barriers to new entrants. What if we applied antitrust policy not just in the private sector but the public sector, too? We saw examples of this in earlier parts of this book—services like schools and healthcare guaranteed by government but competitively provided by the market, through nonprofit or for-profit enterprises.

Now let's apply that thinking to even more of government: open up the provision of public services outright, to all comers. If antitrust policy can help tackle the entrenched power of comfortable elites in the private sector, surely it can have a similar effect in the public sector? If we really want a revolution in government, we need to rethink its role entirely: from provider of services to guarantor of outcomes, delivered in diverse ways by diverse providers. It is a structural reform that would embed entrepreneurialism throughout the public realm. In as many areas of policy as possible, government should be in the business of "buying" the services people demand from it, not "building" them.

Education, discussed in Chapter 2, is perhaps the clearest example of why government should buy, not build. Although of course it's true that there are many high-quality public schools run by the government, it is also self-evidently the case that there are many innovative approaches to education that are denied to America's children because of the government's structural monopoly. Government schools have become factory schools—pretty much the same type of education for every child everywhere—and that's a disastrous way to prepare our young people for the twenty-first century. Of course, government must ensure that every child has access to a decent education, but it can do that by redistributing tax revenue to parents to spend on tuition. Maybe the public school is great and parents will choose to use it. Maybe new competition will spur it to improve. But, far likelier, it won't. And that's okay. Why should we expect government to know how to run a school? Instead of endless bureaucratic efforts to improve failing schools, we should make it easier for new and innovative types of schools to emerge—and compete.

Similarly, do government employees really need to be the ones administering social welfare benefits, or would an entrepreneurial challenger do a better job? Certainly a private real estate portfolio manager would help: in 2014, the General Services Administration was literally unable to account for all the buildings the government owns or leases. Of course, there's one immediate objection people might have about making government services contestable in this way: Didn't we already privatize large swaths of our government? And isn't it hopelessly corrupt? You hear stories all the time from statehouses and city halls around the country about procurement processes rigged by insiders to line the pockets of their friends. It hardly gives reason for confidence. On every level, government-awarded contracts are magnets for bribes, corruption, and cronyism. There is a persistent belief—often well founded—that you have to know someone on the inside to win a bid, so fewer vendors participate, and the benefit of competitive bidding wanes. It's the same old monopolistic provision, just transferred to the private sector with the contractors getting rich in the process.

So it's not enough to simply allow competition. It must also be fair and open, biased toward entrepreneurs, not corrupt establishment cronies. To do that we need to rethink every aspect of the government contracting process to ensure that the barriers that keep insiders protected and insurgent challengers out are torn down. Case in point: when the Health and Human Services Department launched the Obamacare website Healthcare.gov in 2013, practically everything went wrong because the government couldn't manage all the contractors it had hired to construct the site—including the mammoth Booz Allen. Simply put, the system benefited the big companies who can hire armies of lobbyists to help write the procurement contracts and lawyers to navigate the process.

After the Obamacare debacle, *Slate* interviewed Eric Gundersen of Development Seed, who was responsible for the static front-end Web pages that were the only component of the endeavor not to fail. "If I were to bid on the whole project," Gundersen told *Slate*,

"I would need more lawyers and more proposal writers than actual engineers to build the project. Why would I make a company like that?" Is it any surprise that smaller contractors find the bidding to be a rigged system? If antitrust for government is to work, we need to break up contracts into the smallest possible units, outlaw bias in favor of prior contractors, and make the whole process completely open and transparent. There should be no secrets with public money. Yale professor Peter H. Schuck, author of *Why Government Fails So Often: And How It Can Do Better*, writes, "When one compares government and market provision of essentially the same service, the inescapable conclusion is that the market almost always performs more cost-effectively."

So let's do something about it: let's break open the public-sector monopoly and bring a whole new spirit of entrepreneurial innovation to public policy and public services.

3. AMBITIOUS GOVERNMENT

In the end, any entrepreneur will tell you that the most important thing in their business is the people. And the same is true of government. We argue in Chapter 9 that in order to make government more accountable, we need to attract better-quality talent to work there, and pay them more. That's not some vague aspiration: there's a real-world model we can follow: let's treat our public servants like Finnish teachers. Finnish teachers are paid well compared to other professionals, but more important, they're highly respected because everyone understands they were the top performers in a meritocracy. Only one in ten applicants to the teaching profession is accepted in Finland, and they attend a regular university with high standards like other professionals do. The best and brightest want to be teachers, and as a result Finnish students receive superlative educations.

Public-sector unions in the United States, on the other hand, demand specialized credentials to teach, which leads to an industry of "education schools" that water down content so they can find enough qualified candidates to stay in business. Someone willing to limit themselves to a degree from an education school, which isn't applicable to other professional pursuits, is normally committing to a lifetime of teaching whether they enjoy it or not, so he or she can reap the pension earned after paying dues—both literally and figuratively—for twenty years or more.

Right across the public sector, unions make sure that none of their members is paid too little. But in a spirit of leveling, they work to prevent any of their members earning too much, either. By paying for top talent, eliminating the pension incentive that keeps government employees in jobs they are bored by, and by offering them performance bonuses, we could make a difference to the culture inside government and the public sector, bringing a whole new spirit of ambition and dynamism. Singapore is renowned for having the best civil servants in the world: there, you see a small cadre of high-quality officials instead of a sprawling low-quality bureaucracy. If we paid our civil service and politicians the way the market pays private sector employees, would politicians be tempted by Rolexes, golf trips, and football tickets that their accomplished peers working in the private sector can afford, but they can't? If legislative assistants and policy makers earned salaries comparable to private sector peers, wouldn't they bring more experience and expertise to their positions, and need to rely less on lobbyists to explain the content of legislation to them? Singapore also builds accountability into its civil service ranks by awarding cash bonuses linked to the nation's economic performance. Employees are rewarded with several months' salary depending on their performance—not on their education degrees or seniority, to which public-sector unions in the United States peg compensation.

Here's another way of bringing a culture of ambition to government: let's run pilot programs based on the Nobel Prize–winning discovery of "loss aversion," as researchers at the University of Chicago did with teachers who were promised bonuses based on student performance. In 2012 they found that the student performance of a control group was roughly the same as the performance of students whose teachers received traditional bonuses. But students whose teachers were threatened with reduced bonuses for poor performance excelled. Imagine the consequences of a loss-aversion bonus plan for our entire government. America is the land of opportunity. Why not give our civil servants and government workers an open road and the chance to be substantially rewarded for their effectiveness? If it leads to better outcomes, that's good news for working Americans and a populist victory.

Don't get me wrong: our first priority in building the Populist Government should be to get power out of the grabbing, clammy, centralizing hands of our corrupt and incompetent ruling elite and put it in the hands of the people. We make a start on that with a Constitutional Convention to insist on real localism. But we'll still need people to work in our government, at every level. Let's make sure they're the best people, and reward them properly.

IN A NUTSHELL . . .

However much we complain about it, we need government. There will always be some functions run by government, so let's make those agencies and departments more entrepreneurial.

1. Innovative Government: Government should use the principles of human-centered design to provide services that meet people's real needs in a positive way.

2. Antitrust for government: The public sector should set rules and fund services, but shouldn't have a monopoly on providing them; make public agencies compete with nonprofits and companies to drive innovation and results. Reform public procurement to favor outsiders and innovators, not entrenched incumbents.

3. Ambitious government: When government hires people, it should be the best people. Allow public agencies to compete with the private sector on hiring and benefits. Reward civil servants for effectiveness.

9

ACCOUNTABLE

ALTHOUGH IT WAS MARGARET THATCHER'S people-power brand of conservativism that first attracted me to politics, one of my favorite political quotations is from the late Tony Benn—a radical socialist and old-guard Labour leader. Born in 1925, the same year as Thatcher, Benn was a true champion of accountability in government. He attended Oxford University, served in the Royal Air Force during World War II, and grew to become an antiwar activist, vegetarian, and agnostic. When Benn inherited an aristocratic title from his father in the 1960s, he fought successfully to renounce it and remain a commoner. You get the picture. Retiring as a member of Parliament in 2001, Benn gave a final speech in the House of Commons that made a deep impression on me:

"If one meets a powerful person—Adolf Hitler, Joe Stalin or Bill Gates—ask them five questions: 'What power have you got? Where did you get it from? In whose interests do you exercise it? To whom are you accountable? And how can we get rid of you?' If you cannot get rid of the people who govern you, you do not live in a democratic system."

How would the bureaucrats in Brussels, London, or Washington answer those five questions? The elites in Silicon Valley, New York, and Davos? Throughout this book, we have seen examples of public policy distorted to favor the interests of the rich, the well connected, the insiders. That is elitism. And has elitism managed to win over working Americans, the overwhelming majority? There has been too little accountability.

America is the world's oldest democracy, based on the world's best expression of people power, the Constitution, with its astonishingly farsighted and thoughtful framework for citizen-centric governance. And yet despite the Constitution, despite the careful nurturing of its institutions over the past two centuries, American democracy no longer seems to serve "we the people." Today it seems that political legitimacy stems not from votes, but from money or influence: the more of it you have, the more that government pays attention to your concerns. As I wrote in *More Human:* "America, where the rich and powerful literally buy the outcomes they want from the political system, is no longer in any proper sense of the word a democracy, it is a *donocracy.*"

An absolutely vital element of Positive Populism is to fight to make government truly accountable to the people, as it was always intended to be. We need to rein in the bureaucratic Deep State that has taken on authority for itself, with no political legitimacy. But to ensure politicians are accountable, we need to end the stranglehold of big money donors and special interests, whether from the left or the right. Here are some radical ideas for taking our republic back from the elitists who have stolen it.

1. CONFLICT DONORS

When Americans think of corruption, they tend not to think about their own system. After all, with a few exceptions, like the bloviating governor busted for trying to sell President Obama's Senate seat or the odd congressman caught with cash in the freezer, American politics is not outwardly corrupt. But just because it's not so obvious and out in the open as in countries like Russia, China, or Brazil, where officials on government salaries sport fancy watches, drive the latest sports car, and inexplicably have enormous beachfront villas, doesn't mean the American system has no room for corruption. It's quieter, and it's more covert. But it's there, and it's subverting our democracy.

The center of the American donocracy is across the street from Capitol Hill, where members of Congress spend an inordinate amount of time fund-raising from rich donors. Every day they cross the street from their congressional office buildings to the Democratic or Republican congressional campaign buildings (quaintly, one of the few limitations on campaign activity is that they are barred from using government facilities to raise money), where they spend hours making dozens and dozens of calls at a time, pleading for campaign cash for their parties. Is this dignified for a member of the United States *Congress*, the living embodiment of constitutional democracy?

Some members certainly don't think so. Steve Israel, a former Democratic congressman from New York, resigned rather than subject himself any longer to the mandatory self-abasement. In his sixteen years in office, he wrote in the *New York Times*, he "spent roughly 4,200 hours in call time, attended more than 1,600 fundraisers just for my own campaign and raised nearly $20 million in increments of $1,000, $2,500 and $5,000 per election cycle. . . . This is your democracy," he wrote. "But as the bidding grows higher, your voice gets lower. You're simply priced out of the marketplace of ideas. That is, unless you are one of the ultra-wealthy."

That's exactly right. And it's not limited to Congress. For example, in 2014, former Virginia governor Bob McDonnell was convicted on corruption charges by a federal jury for accepting a $6,000 Rolex watch from vitamin businessman Jonnie Williams, as well as a $20,000 New York City shopping spree for his wife, $100,000 in loans to cover his personal debt, and the use of Williams' Ferrari and vacation home. Governor McDonnell was no fool. A common loophole in federal and state laws allows politicians and political appointees to accept limitless gifts that come from "friends"—whether they happen to be lobbyists or not. As the *Los Angeles Times* reported, "Within days, or sometimes within a few minutes, McDonnell responded by calling state officials or sending emails to enlist support for the [vitamin] supplement Williams was promoting."

McDonnell and his wife were ultimately let off due to a technicality—how convenient.

So if such behavior falls—inexplicably—under the category of legal, how can we hold politicians accountable for it? We need a new standard of conduct in politics. Ideally, we would pass the bill once introduced by former Republican congressman David Jolly, who like his colleague Congressman Israel was fed up with the "sweat shop phone booths" where he spent hours each day raising money, "compromis[ing] the dignity of the office." His "Stop Act" would prohibit federal officeholders from soliciting campaign dollars at all. That's a smart and sensible way to curb the temptations of selling influence, or legislation directly. But here's another way to avoid the conflict of interest that flows from the way that politicians raise money—and it doesn't even require legislation. It's a rule change for Congress (and state legislatures, while we're at it), that could be implemented overnight. Let's ban "conflict donors."

Think of "conflict donors" like "conflict diamonds," the ill-begotten diamonds extracted from unstable regions that financed the activities of cash-strapped regimes and militias. Because the locals were casualties of this trade—losing not only their rights but often their lives when forced to mine the gems (or in the conflicts they funded)—conflict diamonds are also known as "blood diamonds," a phrase brought to worldwide attention by the eponymous 2006 movie starring Leonardo DiCaprio and Djimon Hounsou.

Regulation over conflict diamonds is only as good as the norm that accompanied it. Until consumers actively sought to ensure their jewelry was conflict-free, the certification saying so, known as the Kimberly Process, meant nothing.

Similarly with conflict donors, mere laws on the books don't prevent the seedy favor trade pervasive in the halls of power.

So let's set a new standard that voters can easily evaluate: all politicians must recuse themselves from legislative action on any matter that is relevant to any of their donors' interests. No more donations from the banks going to members of the House Financial Services Committee or contributions from health insurers going to senators overseeing healthcare reform or Big Agriculture companies dishing out the cash to the legislators overseeing the farm bill with all its juicy subsidies. And no more of the sickening corruption like that carried out by Republican Speaker of the House John Boehner and his coterie, who would demand money from affected interests for moving forward with legislation that would benefit them—known as "John Boehner's Toll-Booth." All of it is legalized bribery and extortion, plain and simple, and it could be stopped in an instant if members of Congress simply decided en masse that they would no longer work on any matter where they have a conflict donor.

Of course, even as you read those words, you see their objection, don't you? "If I never voted on issues relevant to my donors, then why would they give me any money?" Er yes, exactly. By establishing this new ethical concept—"conflict donors"—we expose the political elite's basic, and endemically corrupt, business model. You get on in Congress by raising money for your party (they call it "dues"). The more you raise, the better your committee assignments. The better your committee assignments, the more effective you will be at delivering for your donors—donors who, of course, are directly affected by the committees you're assigned to. On it goes, the miserable and degrading merry-go-round of money and favors and shameless extortion—sometimes the donor demanding policy for cash, sometimes the politician demanding cash for advancing a policy: all of it rotten to the core, a heartbreaking betrayal of the promise of America's founders.

"A Republic, if you can keep it" became "A Republic, if you can buy it." Now is the time to reform it.

2. EQUAL-ACCESS LOBBYING

It's not just the donations, though. Most public policy that affects the elites is not made in the halls of Congress or state legislatures but in the back offices of administrative agencies. There, unelected bureaucrats make decision after decision that may seem trivial but could be make or break to those directly affected. Far from the bright lights and television cameras of the Capitol, rules are made, interpreted, and enforced by anonymous officials you'll never hear of.

They do have one thing in common with their counterparts on Capitol Hill. In both cases, they rely on lobbyists to inform them, shape policy, and even write the rules and regulations. Overworked and inexperienced (in Congress, the median age of a staffer is thirty-one), these legislative assistants and government bureaucrats all too easily accept the assistance of lobbyists, who so generously offer their time, research, and policy "advice." Of course, it helps that many of those staffers go on to work for the lobbyists themselves. After a few years in government, they are invaluable to deep-pocketed special interests, who hire them to ensure continued access to decision makers, committees, and those same bureaucrats. Whether explicit bribery goes on or not, you can be sure that decisions favor potential future benefactors. This is the famous revolving door between Big Business and Big Government, the seamless transition that is part of the career plan for any aspirant elitist in DC. You slum it for a while in government on a public-sector salary, then cash in when you leave. And then it's back for another stint in government, and so on around the revolving door.

Can we jam it up? We can certainly try. Tighter rules on lobbying could bar lobbyists from being able to write rules or have special access. More effective: place a lifetime ban on government officials working in an industry over which they have had direct oversight. It's also true that reducing the size and scope of government, and decentralizing power along the lines outlined in Chapter 7, would reduce both the need and the opportunity for lobbying and influence-peddling.

A more creative solution, one that's less punitive on the individuals concerned, would be to make it easier to hire the best people and *keep* them in government jobs. To do that, you have to compensate them properly and in line with their performance. Currently the salary of a typical civil servant doesn't depend on job performance or market signals. It is predetermined by an an-timeritocratic government pay scale—probably negotiated by a public-sector union. As a result, the best people are kept out, and the worse are kept in; no rising star wants their promotions and pay tied to arbitrary union rules. As Harvard professor John Do-nahue's seminal book, *The Warping of Government Work,* explains:

> The divergent paths of public and private employment have intensified a long-standing pattern: elite workers spurn public jobs, while less skilled workers cling to government work as a refuge from a harsh private economy. The first trend creates a chronic talent deficit in the public sector. The second trend makes the government workplace rigid and resistant to change. And both contribute to shortfalls in public-sector performance.

Meanwhile, public-sector unions, whose membership now outnumbers private-sector unions in the United States, fortify that "refuge" by making it nearly impossible to fire the employees they protect. As we saw in Chapter 1, private-sector unions can play a positive role in providing economic security for working people. But public-sector unions are a different story. They lobby for laws that force their members to pay them dues; they then spend that money bribing politicians—especially at the state level—to give them inflation-busting raises and guaranteed fat pensions that have blown a devastating hole in many state budgets—most no-tably California's. These cozy deals are negotiated behind closed doors with politicians desperate for the unions' political donations and grassroots support come election time.

If we could loosen the grip of public-sector union contribu-tions on politicians, not only would we be able to shrink the size and cost of government by reducing its bloat, we would be able to incentivize the best and brightest to join government (as we saw in Chapter 8). Perhaps nowhere is this clearer than in public education, where unions keep the barriers to entry high, and reward seniority and certificates instead of performance. It is a total betrayal of public school students who suffer while the elites who make the rules send their own children to private schools where normal market rules prevail.

But in the end, we are not going to stop the practice of lobbying government, and nor should we. Remember the First Amendment, which protects the right "to petition the Government for a redress of grievances." The problem is that the rich and powerful get a vastly disproportionate share of politicians' and civil servants' attention. The goal we should set is Equal-Access Lobbying: require legislators and senior rule-making officials to hold public office hours, managed through an open calendar through which individuals and organizations can book appointments. Any other lobbying contact should be banned.

THERE IS NO SIMPLE ANSWER to the institutionalized corruption of American politics. Goodness knows, many have tried. I'm one of them, with my start-up Crowdpac, a crowdfunding site for politics designed to make it easy for candidates to run for office without relying on the big donors and special interests and party machines. Reforms like banning conflict donors and the revolving door could make a difference; so could structural reforms that decentralize power. But if we really want to make government accountable, there's one more area that the populist revolution needs to target.

3. THE DEEP STATE

Before Tony Blair became the modern face of the British Labour Party in the 1997 elections, its constitution was so dogmatically socialist that it called for "common ownership of the means of production, distribution, and exchange." Blair knew that such a concept was hopelessly outdated in the modern world, and steered the party in a new direction. In crafting the "New Labour" image—friendly to entrepreneurs, reluctant to increase taxes, smarter on crime, he modernized the Labour Party and won three elections in a row. I didn't agree with many of the things Blair did in office. But it had been reported that he became frustrated with the bureaucracy of government as he tried to accelerate his reform program, and so I was interested to see if he had any useful professional advice.

I went with my friend and colleague Rohan Silva to see the former prime minister in 2010. Blair was open and gracious, sharing many valuable insights. But the one thing above all that we remembered was his stark warning about the civil service. In effect, he said, "You cannot overestimate the degree to which the civil service and the bureaucracy genuinely see themselves as the guardians of the national interest. They think it's their duty to block and frustrate the here-today, gone-tomorrow politicians who come in with their crazy schemes. That is how they think. You have to realize that they really are there trying to stop you doing what you want to do. You've got to understand that, and be ready to fight them."

Blair's warning about Britain's Deep State was prophetic, as I discovered even before David Cameron took office as prime minister. One of our key policy pledges was on government transparency. We had promised to publish details of everything the British government spent money on, as well as the names, job descriptions, and the organizational charts of the entire civil service, so citizens could see what their government did. In a meeting ahead of the election, cabinet secretary and head of the civil service Gus O'Donnell asked me and Cameron, "Of course you don't really mean all this government transparency stuff, do you?" When I replied that we very much did, O'Donnell gave me a knowing look and said: "Yes. Well, we'll see about that."

And indeed, once we were in office, the civil service bureaucracy fought tooth and nail against the publication of any information about its scope and functions. And then it dawned on me: Blair was so right. The permanent bureaucracy, self-righteously convinced of its "noble" mission to "protect" the country from democracy, was never going to be an ally in the kind of radical change we were trying to make. The last thing they wanted was to decentralize power—that would mean less power for them.

I saw again what we were up against when I spearheaded the "Red Tape Challenge" in 2010. Every new government comes to office promising to cut bureaucratic red tape. Ours was determined to go further. The prime minister sent all the cabinet ministers a memo urging them to "tackle regulation with vigour," explaining: "There are over 21,000 statutory rules and regulations in force, and I want us to bring that number—and the burden it represents—down. Indeed, I want us to be the first government in modern history to leave office having reduced the overall burden of regulation, rather than increasing it."

To develop specific targets for regulations to cut, we looked to crowdsourcing: We established a month-long comment period for the public to provide feedback on existing rules and regulations, and gave relevant government ministers three months to work out which they wanted to keep and why. At the end of those three months, their staffs came in to a series of meetings with huge binders of regulations pertaining to their departments, flagged with green, yellow, and red tabs. The number of red tabs far exceeded the number of green and yellow tabs, which at first glance I found encouraging. That's because I wrongly assumed the red tabs signaled the red tape they were ready to cut. In fact, it was the opposite. The red tabs were the rules the civil servants were recommending we keep—the overwhelming majority of rules and regulations on the books! The exercise wasn't a total failure: we did manage to get rid of some of the most pointless regulation. But it was a huge battle, because the bureaucrats—or "bumocrats," as the Beatles' John Lennon famously called them—were behaving just as Tony Blair warned us they would.

That's when I realized that there was no way we were going to be able to truly decentralize power and make government more accountable unless we actually bit the bullet and cut back the size of the bureaucracy—drastically. I had an idea: For centuries, the British Empire was run out of Somerset House, a magnificent, palatial complex on the Thames, not far from Trafalgar Square. Here were the offices of the empire's civil servants. In the colonial era, when "the sun never set on the British Empire" because it spanned the globe, the offices ruled territory from Australia and New Zealand to Africa, India and the Middle East, and across the Atlantic to Canada. In addition to all those charges, Great Britain administered all of Ireland and Scotland as well.

"How many staff worked at Somerset House?" I inquired. The answer? Roughly 10,000. Well: if Britain could preside over the largest empire in world history from one building that housed 10,000 people, why couldn't modern Britain, which had no empire to administer? Why was it necessary for Whitehall (the core civil service in London) to be staffed by well over 100,000 people? Using Somerset House as a guideline, I proposed an experiment:

to cut the central civil service bureaucracy by 90 percent for a few years, and to evaluate the impact. To me it was the logical corollary of our plan to decentralize power. If we really meant that, we would need fewer bureaucrats at the center, surely? As you can imagine, this plan did not go down well with either the political or bureaucratic establishment: the elites never want to give up power.

But they must give up power—or have it taken away from them—if we are to make government truly accountable to the people.

The federal bureaucracy in Washington—the American Deep State—is sorely in need of just such a radical shakeup. In 2017, the US civil service consisted of nearly three million taxpayer-funded jobs. Anyone who has been to Washington has seen in one city block after another the sprawling physical landscape of bureaucracy. But what exactly do they all do in there? Many must do important work. But let's find out exactly what. Let's open them up to scrutiny and hold them to account. It's our tax dollars, after all.

Let's start by bringing into the open the secret world of the administrative state. Publish every civil service organization chart, along with salaries and job descriptions. That will provide the necessary intelligence for establishing the scale of reduction we need. In the process, let's clear out all the leeches and hangers-on—the useless elitist management consultants who earn a fortune from the taxpayer from writing endless PowerPoint presentations for incoming administrations that do nothing but perpetuate the vast, corrupt cronyism of the Washington, DC, swamp. The result is a self-satisfied ruling class of mandarins stuck in acronyms, cost-analysis reports, and legal jargon. Hardly the government "of, by, and for the people" that the framers had in mind.

Cutting the size of the bureaucracy would be a gigantic step in the right direction, but that's just the start of a true accountability plan for government. Without constraints, bureaucracy always has, and always will, run amok, a self-perpetuating kraken-like monstrosity. Historically speaking, we once tolerated bureaucracy as the "necessary evil" in order to achieve scale and efficiency of government. In a pre-digital age, there was simply no other way to fairly and effectively administer a large country. But once the ball started rolling, bureaucracy begot more bureaucracy; government grew larger and more distant, even when it didn't have to.

The sad part is that this one-directional (that is, ever-growing) approach to the size and scope of bureaucracy is a relatively new phenomenon. As little as fifty years ago, government's size and scope waxed and waned as public policy challenges arose and were addressed. According to political scientists James Q. Wilson and John DiIulio,

> The Old System had a small agenda. . . . When someone proposed adding a new issue to the public agenda, a major debate often arose over whether it was legitimate for the federal government to take action at all in the matter. . . . For the government to take bold action under this system, the nation usually had to be facing a crisis. . . . Each succeeding crisis left the government bureaucracy somewhat larger than it had been before, but when the crisis ended, the exercise of extraordinary powers ended. . . . The New System . . . is characterized by a large policy agenda, the end of the debate over the legitimacy of government action (except in the area of First Amendment freedoms), the diffusion and decentralization of power in Congress, and the multiplication of interest groups. . . . Under the Old System, the checks and balances made it difficult for the government to start a new program, and so the govern-

ment remained relatively small. Under the New System, these checks and balances make it hard to change what the government is already doing, and so the government remains large.

How accurate—and utterly depressing. It also heightens the importance of the accountability question. How can an ever-larger bureaucracy answer to a (relatively) stable small number of political appointees? It can't. And as a result, unelected, unconstrained bureaucrats exercise enormous amounts of illegitimate power with little to no democratic oversight. Whether you agree with it or not, surely it is right that any new rule or regulation should be signed off by someone democratically accountable to the voters either directly or indirectly through congressional oversight and confirmation.

But because of the inexorable growth of the federal bureaucracy, hundreds of rules are made and enforced without even the rubber-stamp approval of a congressionally confirmed political appointee. This isn't just wrong, it's unconstitutional. According to academics Todd Gaziano and Tommy Berry: "The attempted delegation of rulemaking authority to someone not appointed as an 'Officer of the United States' violates one of the most important separation-of-powers clauses in the Constitution." They added in the *Wall Street Journal*, "A career bureaucrat shouldn't have the power to disrupt thousands of lives." They found that one civil servant at the Department of Health and Human Services had signed nearly two hundred rules—without bothering to get the approval of any political appointees.

While unaccountable bureaucratic action can sometimes be an appropriate way to exercise power (in cases where technical expertise or nonpolitical impartiality is needed), in practice most of the time it simply cannot be justified. The modern administrative state has developed a notion of bureaucratic accountability, where anonymous civil servants or obscure processes produce results that are imposed on citizens. That is simply wrong: in place of bureaucratic accountability, we should have democratic accountability, where the decision that affects your life can be traced back to someone who can answer Tony Benn's five questions—the ones we opened this chapter with—affirmatively.

What power have you got? Where did you get it from? In whose interests do you exercise it? To whom are you accountable? And how can we get rid of you?

We need that kind of spirit in America today: not just fewer civil servants, but a bureaucracy that behaves in an accountable way, supporting the political process and not subverting it. In part, judicial appointments can help fight back the power grab of the unaccountable administrative state. But this battle needs to be a prominent public contest, too.

These questions of civil service reform, curbs on political donations, and lobbying: they may not grab the headlines and dominate public debate. But they are essential steps on the road toward true Populist Government. One of the most important ways in which the elitists hold on to power is their intimate understanding of the corrupt and unaccountable system they have designed for themselves. Yelling "Drain the swamp!" is the right sentiment, but no substitute for a strategy. It will not deliver the revolution we need. Instead we must learn how the system works and undermine it from within. That's the way to move America decisively in the direction of more accountable government and real people power.

IN A NUTSHELL . . .

Americans are rightly disgusted by the rampant corruption and cynical lack of accountability that pervades their politics and government. Piecemeal reform isn't enough: it's time for a political revolution to undermine the structures that support elitism.

1. **Ban Conflict Donors:** All politicians must recuse themselves from legislative action on any matter that is relevant to a donor's interests.

2. **Equal-Access Lobbying:** Institute open office hours for politicians and policy-making officials; all other contacts should be banned.

3. **Defeat the Deep State:** The Federal bureaucracy is too big and too remote from the people it serves; let's cut it down by 90 percent and distribute as many of those functions as possible out of Washington. Publish the names, job descriptions, and salaries of every civil servant to help plan an all-out assualt on the unaccountable administrative state and make a reality of "drain the swamp."

CONCLUSION

FOR DECADES, ELITISTS have promised working people everything: higher wages, bigger homes, better education for their children, affordable healthcare, and a strong national defense. You'll do better than your parents, they've promised, and your children will do better than you.

The elites have fulfilled those promises—for themselves. They've built their children glorious schools, created the best healthcare system in the world for their parents, and watched their wages and wealth climb without limit. But did they notice that in recent decades, for most people—around 80 percent of people— those promises were not delivered? Did they stop to listen, to observe, to take in the criticism? To perhaps slow down the growth of their bureaucracies, or halt the creeping centralization of power into *their* hands?

No. They held on, no matter what.

It's no wonder that a populist cry has gone up in Western

democracies in recent years. From Britain to Italy, Germany to America, the people have had enough of the self-serving, self-righteous elitists who expect working people to sacrifice so they can buy second homes.

The voters who have rebelled against this sclerotic order should be saluted, congratulated, and encouraged. But there is a dark shadow overhanging the populist awakening. In addition to its well-deserved criticism of the elites and the establishment, the populist movement has too often become distracted with well-founded anger channeled into rage rather than reason.

My populism is positive, open, and productive. It is patriotic and generous. I cannot bear to see it hijacked by a hateful few. Populism doesn't equal racism, or xenophobia, or bigotry. Yes, populists cast blame—and rightly so. But positive populists also ask how to help.

SO LET'S NOT APPEAL to people's worst impulses rather than their best. Let's not unite people in fear and anger. Let's bring them together for greater purpose. There is a long, proud tradition of populism in America. Not all of it is good, of course. But populism gave rise to this country, and has sustained it ever since. Each generation of Americans has fulfilled the legacy of the Founding Fathers with its own American revolution. Populists peopled the West, extinguished slavery, and fought for women's suffrage. They won two world wars, established civil rights, and built the greatest economy in the history of the world.

But we've lost that momentum. We've let the centralizers and the bureaucrats get the better of us. The elitists think they know how to run your life, but they don't: *you* do. Whether through more parental control of education, more competition in key sectors of the economy, or more decision making at the local level, the ideas in this book are united by a single principle: putting power in people's hands, in *your* hands.

The populist movement has the potential to be the next revolution to renew this country. But it must be constructive. And it must be positive.

ACKNOWLEDGMENTS

By the time my previous book, *More Human*, was published in America, I remember telling a friend that I wasn't really satisfied with it. It missed the extraordinary political moment we were living through—the disruption of traditional politics that Brexit, Bernie Sanders, Donald Trump, and others represented. "I'm going to have to write another book to make the argument I really want to make," I said.

The thought of it horrified me, but two years on, I can barely believe how smooth the process has been. For that I have to thank a relatively small but highly talented group of people. First of all, the Crown Forum team: Mary Reynics, Tina Constable, Campbell Wharton, Ashley Hong, Megan Perritt, Nicole McArdle, Philip Leung, Cathy Hennessy, Jen Valero, and others at Penguin Random House who brought the book to fruition. From my perspective, at least, it has been an incredibly straightforward and enjoyable experience. The fact that from our very first meeting we had a clear and shared understanding of what we were aiming for made a huge difference.

My test for this book was that I should be able to write it without my wife, Rachel, and two sons, Ben and Sonny, noticing—and that goal was pretty much achieved. As ever, I want to thank them for everything: I can't imagine life without you. I love you so much.

The book would quite simply never have become a reality without Bernadette Peters. I can't thank you enough for helping to get the show on the road, and for helping me to see how important it is to bring a personal dimension to policy arguments.

Scott Bade: not a coauthor this time—as you were with *More Human*—but thanks for all your help, not least in those moments of techno-panic as I juggled the word-processing products of our various tech behemoths.

Speaking of tech, and juggling: a heartfelt thanks to all my former colleagues and investors at my start-up, Crowdpac. I know it was not easy to handle my political views in these hyperpolarized times, but I'm incredibly proud of what we built together and will always be grateful for the chance to do it with you.

I want to thank Keith Urbahn and the team at Javelin for all their wise advice and brilliant support, and of course for introducing me to the team at Crown. And thank you, Juleanna Glover, for introducing me to Keith.

Rupert Murdoch has given me the most extraordinary opportunity for a new career, one that is as much of a surprise to me as it is to everyone who knows me, and I am enormously grateful. I have loved being part of the Fox News family—everyone I've met and worked with has been so warm and kind and professional. There are too many to list here, but I do especially want to thank my brilliant team and crew on *The Next Revolution*, in Los Angeles and New York.

Peggy Noonan: getting to know you has been one of the great joys of moving to America. Thank you for your warmth and wisdom—and for allowing me to shamelessly steal the phrase "positive populism" from one of your columns. But then you got it from John Kasich, so I guess that's OK—thanks, John!

Finally, my love and thanks to Rohan Silva, for encouraging me, supporting me, reading and commenting on the first draft—for everything. I'm so proud of you, and so lucky to have you as my friend.

ABOUT THE AUTHOR

Steve Hilton is host of *The Next Revolution* on Fox News, and an entrepreneur and former senior policy advisor in the UK government. Since moving to the United States in 2012, he has taught at Stanford University and founded a nonpartisan political technology start-up with the mission of fighting big money in politics and putting power in people's hands. He is the author of *More Human: Designing a World Where People Come First*, a *Sunday Times* (UK) bestseller in 2015. He lives in the San Francisco Bay Area with his wife and two sons. And ten chickens.